MENANDER

DYSKOLOS, SAMIA AND OTHER PLAYS

A Companion to the Penguin Translation of the
Plays of Menander by Norma Miller

Stanley Ireland

Published by Bristol Classical Press
General Editor: John H. Betts

First published in 1992 by
Bristol Classical Press
an imprint of
Gerald Duckworth & Co. Ltd
61 Frith Street
London W1D 3JL
e-mail: inquiries@duckworth-publishers.co.uk
Website: www.ducknet.co.uk

Reprinted 2001

A catalogue record for this book is available
from the British Library

ISBN 1-85399-199-6

Printed in Great Britain by
Antony Rowe Ltd, Eastbourne

1005054646

In Memory of Norma Miller

Contents

Introduction

'Menander has so blended his diction that it suits every nature, every disposition, every age.' With these words Plutarch (Moralia 853f.) summed up antiquity's assessment of Menander's poetic skill as outstanding in its facility and unaffected air. It is a verdict we might equally apply to many other aspects of his dramatic art; for there is much in Menander's works that testifies to his ability to disguise sophistication of technique with an aura of naturalness and even inevitability. Common sense tells us, of course, that there is nothing truly natural in a play, nothing that occurs of its own accord. Instead, everything is the product of the playwright's mind and invention. As a result, the greater the cohesion between events, the greater the evidence for his skill.

A stage may be reached, however, when the action appears so natural to a cursory glance that it seems banal. One of the prime aims of this commentary, therefore, is to make accessible to students the scale of Menander's sophistication that lies beneath the veneer of inevitability, and to suggest that repeated reading will bring with it the reward of ever-deepening insights. There is, of course, a limit to how much can be included within the format of a work such as this, and compared to the amount of literature that scholars have produced the pages that follow might well be thought hardly to scratch the surface. Nevertheless I have tried to provide readers with as much information as possible on those plays of which substantial sections remain. If at times my argument appears over-condensed and language contorted, I can only plead the constraints of space and the need to outline those areas of contention which still exist. For those with access to a large library I have provided some indication of further reading, almost all of which is in English. I have also tried to take account of the no less voluminous literature on the plays in other languages and to incorporate the substance of this into the commentary.

One of the major difficulties in dealing with literary works that are fragmentary, as most of Menander's are, is the uncertainty that this injects into any analysis of developments. The greater the fragmentation the greater the uncertainty, as *The Sikyonian* or *The Man She Hated* reveal

1

only too well. Our ignorance of who speaks certain lines or even which characters are involved in some of the scenes opens up an almost limitless permutation of possible scenarios, which even the most careful translation, as that of Norma Miller undoubtedly is, must at times gloss over. On occasion, too, the analysis of passages is founded on isolated words or even mere groupings of letters that no translation can hope to make intelligible. In such cases I have presented ideas in either a simplified form or have suggested solutions without being able to provide in full the evidence upon which they are based.

Throughout the preparation of this work I have enjoyed, and even come to rely upon, the encouragement and advice of Professor W.G. Arnott of Leeds University. Time and again he has pointed out the deficiencies of my argument or the possibility of other interpretations. To him, therefore, I owe a great debt of gratitude. Needless to say, whatever faults remain are entirely my own.

Bibliographical Note
Superscript numbers in the text refer to entries in the bibliography e.g., Sandbach[1] refers to Sandbach's first bibliographical entry.

Old Cantankerous

Act I

Pan's opening monologue, which forms the prologue to the play, has as its main purpose exposition: setting the scene, introducing the characters and establishing the situation at the beginning of the action. To the modern theatre-goer such a device may appear blatantly artificial, but in an ancient context it formed an economic means of conveying information without what Sandbach[1] aptly describes (p. 133) as 'the difficulty of smuggling into the dialogue facts needed more for the audience's sake than for that of the characters'.

Since the prime function of the prologue is to convey information, the playwright must first capture and then retain the audience's attention. To do this Pan exists only partially within the dramatic illusion, the pretence that what the audience sees is real; hence the blatant audience address of the opening words. Thereafter the prologue displays a greater element of formal structure and planning than is immediately evident in the action proper. So for instance, as in the tragedies of Euripides, significant words in the Greek text are often placed at the two important positions within lines: their beginnings and ends, as is the case with *Attica, Phyle, Phyleans, Knemon, Pan* and the verbal echoes of *company*. Structurally, too, the prologue shows careful planning, with Knemon himself in the title role at its centre, surrounded by the description of the setting and the love element. Within this too there is a distinct contrast between country and city themes, mirrored in the actual order in which characters are introduced. As Ramage observes, Knemon and Kallipides, the first and last to be mentioned, form an outer frame within which the relationships of Gorgias, the daughter and Sostratos are themselves developed.

Though typical of much of New Comedy, the prologue was not the invariable format for introducing such information. The same function in other plays might be fulfilled by a dialogue, such as that between the slaves Tranio and Grumio in Plautus' *The Ghost*. Even where there was a prologue, it might not form the opening scene, but be deferred to a later position, as in Menander's *The Shield*. Similarly, the deliverer of a prologue need not

3

invariably be a god in the traditional mould; in *The Rape of the Locks* we find instead the personified abstraction Misapprehension, who, like Chance in *The Shield*, was often elevated to divine status and regarded as a controlling factor in human affairs. One function, however, shared by most plays containing a super-human prologue-speaker was the revelation of some important fact unknown to the humans involved. This allowed the development of New Comedy's major effect, dramatic irony: where the audience's superior knowledge enabled it to appreciate the mistakes and embarrassment of the stage characters. Does this, however, apply in the present case? Is there anything that Pan really contributes that is unknown to the humans involved, or would a human prologue speaker, such as Moschion in *The Girl from Samos*, have been equally possible? Many commentators have questioned whether the use of a god is justified simply by his ability to introduce characters and divinely inspire Sostratos' love. Pan does, however, serve as an effective means of inserting details in a number of respects:

1) At the beginning of the play it is only Pan who can introduce *all* the major characters.

2) The god's objective view allows Knemon's misanthropy to be seen from the start as part of his character and not merely a symptom of madness as Pyrrhias believes, or of transient ill-temper as Chaireas concludes.

3) The divine inspiration for Sostratos' love enables the playwright to develop the theme of natural justice – in this case an advantageous marriage as a reward for piety (36-9 cf. Plautus' *The Pot of Gold* 23ff.) – which runs through many New Comedy plots.

4) Pan's role introduces further dramatic irony throughout the action by later, apparently irrelevant, references to the god and Sostratos' tendency to appropriate to himself responsibility for bringing about a marriage to which he has in fact contributed so little (see further Goldberg[1], Zagagi[2] p. 84ff.).

2. Phyle: A village close to the border with Boeotia, and hence remote from Athens, an appropriate situation for a character like Knemon.

5. on my right: The audience's left and by convention the side which in an urban stagesetting would lead characters away from the city to foreign parts. Thus, of the three buildings on the stage Knemon's is pointedly the farthest from Athens.

6. Knemon: It is not by chance that apart from Pan the old man is the only character actually named in the prologue, thereby emphasising his central role. All others are identified by their roles alone, an understandable feature in a genre which relied so heavily upon stock characters, and designed to avoid overcrowding the play's opening with details before they become relevant, cf. Chrysis in *The Girl from Samos*, Kleostratos in *The Shield*. Throughout the action indeed Knemon is presented as such an unapproachable figure that some commentators have been tempted to see the play's theme as dual and not single, and to elevate development of the old man's character to an importance equal to that of the love intrigue. This, however, is to misunderstand the function of Knemon, and the impression of a lack of integration of themes stems directly from the nature of his depiction.

11. passing my door: cf. 433f. Theocritus *Idyll* I 15ff. aptly describes the unpleasant consequences of angering Pan: 'It is not right, oh shepherd, it is not right for us at midday to play the pipe. Pan it is we fear; for at that time in weariness from the chase he takes his rest, and he is quick-tempered and bitter wrath forever sits upon his nose.' The result of catching the god unawares or failing to greet him could, in fact, be *panic*.

14. he did get married: Marriage constitutes an illogical action for the anti-social Knemon, as Pan is at pains to point out, but is necessary for the plot; the illogicality is further minimised by the subsequent history of the marriage.

20. that just made things worse: The girl, instead of uniting her parents, drove them further apart – female offspring offered less promise of an economic return in terms of work when they grew up, could not carry on the family line, and needed to be provided with a dowry on marriage.

27. growing up now: The term used by Menander might cover the whole age range from 14 to 21, but is more specifically found in the context of the 18-21 age-group, and it is doubtless this that is meant here. Menander aptly closes his initial sketch of Gorgias with a general observation on the maturing effect of responsibility and hard work, the latter being an important theme that runs throughout the play and forms a major point of contrast between the rural and urban characters. For instance, work forms a major element in the next section, dealing with the development of Knemon's character (30ff.). Similarly, it is while Daos is going to join his master, who is digging his land, that he sees Sostratos talking to the girl (207ff.). It is also by Sostratos' willingness to engage in manual labour (370ff.) in order to attract the attention of Knemon and thereby create a good impression, that he bridges the gulf between his pampered upbringing and being deemed worthy in Gorgias' eyes of winning his bride; and it is digging that Pan imposes on the young man in his mother's dream (416f.), thereby arranging for the presence of Sostratos' family at the shrine at just the right moment to cause the old man's accident, and allow Sostratos to reap the benefit of his altered view of life.

31. an old servant woman: Note how Simiche's existence is introduced almost as an afterthought, minimising its potential for diminishing Knemon's solitary life.

33. the suburbs of Athens: lit. 'Cholargos', a city deme on the north side of Athens beyond the Kerameikos.

35. has turned out as you'd expect from her upbringing: That Knemon's daughter should be described as 'innocent and good' because of her upbringing has caused no small surprise among commentators. However, what Menander emphasises here and elsewhere in the play (384ff.) is the beneficial effect of an upbringing isolated from the corrupting influences of society in general, cf. Xenophon *Oeconomicus* VII 5f., in which Ischomachus declares with satisfaction that before their marriage his wife had been raised 'so that she might see as little as possible, hear as little as possible and ask as little as possible'.

41. lives in town: In this way Menander avoids the illogicality of Sostratos not having seen Knemon's daughter before, or of not knowing Knemon's reputation despite the fact that his father, Kallipides, has an estate nearby.

46. and please do like: This forms the *captatio benevolentiae*, the appeal for the audience's favour in what was, after all, a dramatic contest between playwrights.

50ff.: Just as the prologue set out the situation from the standpoint of Pan's superior knowledge, so the first scene of the action proper is equally expository: showing the consequences of the god's intervention from the human standpoint, and forming the basis for the initial depiction of Sostratos and his tendency to rely upon the efforts of others. Technically, Chaireas is a *protatic* character, introduced into the opening scenes of the play specifically for the purpose of exposition, but who thereafter disappears from the action. However, Menander skilfully imposes an apt set of characteristics onto the stock figure of Chaireas, which allows him to be contrasted, first with Sostratos, in the latter's demands for instant results, and later with Gorgias, in the effectiveness of the assistance actually given. Such indeed is the picture of Chaireas created by the playwright that the later compiler of the List of Characters prefacing the Greek text styled him a *parasite*: someone who attached himself to the wealthy and made a living through flattery and the provision of minor services to them, or, as Handley[1] puts it (p. 140), 'a member of the class who make friendship a profession, cultivating their social superiors for their own advantage'. The appropriateness of such a description, however, depends much upon whether we view Chaireas in terms of strict logic or accept, as Menander doubtless intended, the subjective reactions of Sostratos himself as essentially objective (see further 126f. n.).

What?: The entry of the pair as if in mid-conversation, signalled by

Chaireas' opening words, was a common technique of Menander's char-
acter-introduction, cf. 233. Frost (p. 10f.) differentiates four methods
employed in the convention:

1) a question referring to previous offstage dialogue, as here;

2) use of opening gambits such as 'Well' (*The Shield* 250), 'But if...'
(*The Arbitration* 714);

3) reference to earlier dialogue by quotation (*The Rape of the Locks*
1006);

4) context (*Old Cantankerous* 611, 784, *The Arbitration* 218).

51f. putting garlands...fell in love at first sight: Menander injects
an early reminder of the close connection between the girl's piety and its
reward, but one which, through Chaireas' surprise at the speed of Sostratos' emotional attachment, allows the young man to stress the sincerity
of his love on a purely human level.

56. a practical man: The description encapsulates the first point of
dichotomy between Sostratos' expectations and the reality of Chaireas'
assistance, which is now detailed. Both scenarios developed by Chaireas
in 58ff. are, in fact, clearly inappropriate to Sostratos' present situation,
as the young man's reaction in 68f. indicates. The first involves a call-girl
– in all likelihood a slave owned by a pimp, such as the one abducted by
Aeschinus in Terence's *The Brothers*, after he had burst into her owner's
home in the manner here described. The second scenario, though centred
on marriage, is clearly irrelevant to a young man who shows himself
uninterested in the finer points of an arranged match such as that meant
here, where considerations of the girl's actual character are of less importance than social status and finance. Indeed Chaireas' careful self-description and his whole attitude towards Sostratos' situation, like his later
reaction to the picture of Knemon given by Pyrrhias, reveal him as something of a schemer, someone given to a careful weighing up of pertinent
factors, who opts for safety and certainty – all unsuitable for a situation
that demands the taking of chances.

60. burn the door down: This forms part of the conventional behaviour of the ardent lover seeking to gain access to his mistress, cf. Theocritus *Idyll* II 127ff.: 'But if you rejected me and a bolt held the door,
axes and torches would have advanced against you on every side.'.

71. I sent Pyrrhias: Again Sostratos indicates his tendency to rely
upon the efforts of others, and, as Chaireas' reaction indicates, the choice
of a slave to serve as negotiator for establishing contact in a marriage suit
is singularly inept.

78. I can't think what's keeping him: Sostratos' impatience is
hardly appropriate since Pyrrhias gives no evidence of slowness in
carrying out his orders. It does, however, prepare for the slave's entry, a
method Sandbach[1] describes as 'somewhat artless', though it was in fact

7

a standard dramatic device, cf. Sophocles' *Oedipus Tyrannos* 289, Frost p.11f. In addition, this same impatience becomes one of Sostratos' major characteristics in the course of the action, as he constantly strives for instant success (cf. Zagagi[2] p.80ff.).

81. Pyrrhias: The bustle of the slave's entry with his cries to clear the way is reminiscent of the running slave of later Comedy, though with the difference that the latter is motivated by a desire to deliver news to his master, while Pyrrhias here is spurred on from behind (cf. W.S. Anderson[1]), his panic serving to establish the emotional atmosphere of the coming scene and to provide the audience with confirmation of Knemon's character.

101f. wild pears...back: Commentators have made various, and often fantastic, attempts to see some logical significance in the rather obscure Greek with which Pyrrhias describes Knemon's behaviour here. Since it is clear from 121, however, that Knemon was indeed collecting pears, probably from the ground, Pyrrhias, with a slave's experience of hard work, is only too ready to equate this with later trouble. Into a situation already marked by the incongruity of Chaireas' expertise and Sostratos' demands, the slave now ushers in another contrast: between his own pointed attempt to be tactful and the reaction this provokes from Knemon. Within this we see yet another contrast as Chaireas' response changes from irony to evident alarm, while Sostratos' refusal to follow advice and retreat (123) is later to be reversed quite radically when he is confronted by the old man himself.

126f. Put off your visit to him: The superior knowledge of the audience shows Chaireas' reaction here to be totally misguided, though perfectly logical in terms of the information available to him. What Pyrrhias has encountered is not a temporary aberration but a basic characteristic, so that the advice to wait for a more opportune moment and the promise of help in the future cannot but prove ultimately futile. In the event, however, Chaireas is never given the chance either to put his promise of assistance into practice or to realise his mistaken interpretation of events: his role is soon to be taken over in fact by Gorgias, who proves to be far more 'practical' a friend. The picture of Chaireas we are left with, that of a fair-weather friend, is further bolstered by Sostratos' outpouring of peeved frustration (136ff.) born of Chaireas' failure to react appropriately to the young man's impatience. To produce his effect, therefore, Menander has combined our superior knowledge of the situation, together with Sostratos' wholly subjective outburst, to create in our minds an impression of failure without the actual substance. In any case, Chaireas' primary role – eliciting information – is one severely limited in its potential for development, and having been fully exploited, his very exit with its lack of any clear exit line serves as much to characterise Sostratos as it does himself.

139. God rot you entirely: Further characterisation of Sostratos. Disappointed in his hopes of help from Chaireas, he now vents his irritation on the only other character present, with the clearly unjustified and illogical charge that Pyrrhias, although sent to make a good impression, did something to arouse Knemon's anger. In making his charge Sostratos in fact shows himself to be as incapable of accepting the extreme reality of the old man as Chaireas had been. Soon, however, faced with Knemon himself (145ff.) Sostratos shows his true colours as his courage deserts him – his ready confession of fear (151) both confirming Knemon's awesomeness and reinforcing the picture of the young man as incapable of acting for himself. That Sostratos should lose his nerve is, of course, dramatically necessary; if the theme of Knemon as the obstacle to the marriage is to be developed to the full, the two cannot as yet be brought into any meaningful contact. Moreover, Menander's portrayal of Knemon is so extreme that he could hardly have avoided making the old man's reaction to any attempt by Sostratos to broach the subject of marriage the same as that meted out to Pyrrhias – unacceptable behaviour towards someone destined to become his son-in-law.

153ff. Knemon: The unsociable picture of Knemon, prepared for in the previous scene, is now reinforced by the monologue that marks his entry onto the stage, presenting as it does the encounter with Pyrrhias from quite a different angle. Employment of such allegorical introductions – the reference to Perseus, able to fly because of winged sandals given by Hermes, and armed with the severed head of the Gorgon, Medusa, which turned all who looked on it to stone – is not in fact uncommon, finding parallels not only elsewhere in Menander (fr. 535 'Well aren't they right to depict Prometheus chained to the rocks...'), but also in Aristophon (fr. 11 'Well, wasn't it right and proper that Love was expelled by the twelve gods...'), Antiphanes (fr. 159 'Well, aren't the Scythians very wise...'), and Plautus (*Bacchides* 925ff. 'They say the Atreidae did a great deed when they laid low Priam's city of Troy...' cf. Zagagi[1] p. 29ff.). At the same time the development of his complaint begins the process of revealing Knemon's antisocial behaviour as derived not from misanthropy pure and simple, but from an exaggerated desire for isolation, cf. 169f., 597, 694ff.

166. hordes of them: Knemon's tendency to turn minor irritation into a major inconvenience, like his use of plural verbs in the context of Sostratos at 173 ('you and your friends'), 175 ('make a date', 'if you want'), 176 ('put up a bench'), is only part of the subtle linguistic technique by which Menander characterises the old man. In addition, for instance, there is his tendency to see everything in terms of black and white, or, more properly, in terms of all and nothing: 'never' (155), 'no shortage', 'all round here' (158f.), cf. 'nothing' (507), 'from any of you'

9

(513), 'not a soul to help' (598), 'never need' (714), 'never' (720, 724ff., 735); (see further Arnott[3] p.147,[11] p. 30).

173. public walk-way: A Stoa or covered colonnade where people could meet for a variety of purposes. One of them, the Stoa Poikile or Painted Stoa in Athens, gave its name to the Stoic philosophy, since it was there that its founder, Zeno, was in the habit of propounding his ideas.

181f. Should I go and fetch Getas?: True to type, following his débacle with Knemon, Sostratos reverts to his reliance upon others, this time the slave Getas, the description of whom is reminiscent of the later cunning slave character of Roman comedy, habitually employed to get his young master out of a tight corner (cf. Tranio in Plautus' *The Ghost*). As we eventually see, however, Sostratos' expectations of him as a 'real ball of fire' prove as ill-founded as his earlier assessment of Chaireas' practicality.

188. there's the door: This forms a conventional reference to either the creaking of the hinges as the door was being opened, or the rattling of the catch, and was used to suggest the entry of a character from one of the stage houses. It is first found in Euripides, and by Menander's time had clearly become a standard convention cf. 204 ('What was that noise?'), 586, 689, *The Arbitration* 875, 906, *The Girl from Samos* 300, 532, 567, 669, *The Rape of the Locks* 316, Bader, Frost p. 6f.

189: The entry of the girl brings with it a tone of seriousness linked via the well with the theme that will bring about Knemon's change of mind. As Goldberg[2] p. 77f. observes, however, this is juxtaposed with the evident comic nature of Sostratos' asides.

190f. she's dropped the bucket down the well: Ancient wells were generally not fitted with a windlass so that the bucket, or, more properly a two-handled pot, would be lowered and raised directly by hand, thus offering the opportunity for letting slip the rope to which it was attached. In this seemingly casual manner Menander introduces a theme that is to lead ultimately to the situation through which Sostratos wins his bride. The girl's evident fluster at being caught unprepared indicates that Knemon has clearly left off work early because of the encounter with Pyrrhias.

194. Ladies and Gentlemen: lit. 'Gentlemen'. Menander does not include women in such references, though we can hardly doubt their presence, not least because of the themes he introduces into his plays. Technically the exclamation ruptures the dramatic illusion: the conventional pretence that what the audience sees is real, but in the context of the ancient theatre, with no means of darkening the auditorium or of spotlighting the stage, the presence of the audience was always a more obvious factor than today. Even so, instances of the device in Menander are nowhere as blatant as Roman comedy was later to make them (cf. Plautus' *The Pot of Gold* 715ff.).

198f. I don't want to disturb them: The girl's reluctance to get water from the shrine is quite in keeping with the picture of her already built up, i.e., as deeply reverential to the gods and shy of others as a result of her isolated upbringing. Indeed, despite the smallness of her dramatic role Menander imbues her with a considerable depth of character. Her reluctance to enter the shrine, of course, also forms a natural cue for the intervention of Sostratos.

202ff. Great God...that noise: Menander here introduces a subtle juxtaposed description of the young couple: the one overjoyed, the other apprehensive.

205. I'll catch it if he finds me out here: Yet another perspective on the character of Knemon: even his closest kin is afraid of him. Linked with this is her concern for the old serving woman in 195f. It is remarkable in fact how vivid a picture Menander establishes within the space of only a few lines.

206. Daos: The entry onto the stage of a new character so close to the end of the Act is not a momentary lapse on the part of the playwright but a deliberate device to unite Acts and minimise the divisions created by the intervention of the chorus, cf. the entry of Sikon and Getas at the end of Act II, or of Kallipides in Act IV, Turner[1] p. 11. From the information given by Pan in the Prologue, Daos is of course addressing Gorgias' mother inside the house. This technique of a newly arrived character continuing to address someone still inside is in fact specifically designed to add an air of naturalness to the entry, cf. 456, 487, 546, 874, Frost p. 7f.

209. Poverty: The personification of poverty as one of the ills afflicting mankind was an established commonplace by Menander's time. In the sixth century BC the lyric poet Alcaeus had written 'Grievous is Poverty, evil ungovernable, who with her sister Helplessness, subdues a great people' (trans. Page), while the idea of her as a constant resident is found in the elegiac poet Theognis 351ff.: 'Ah, wretched Poverty, why do you delay leaving to go to some other home?'

212: The girl's exit without a word of thanks is, according to Frost p. 45, evidence of her embarrassment at having Daos witness her contact with Sostratos. It might equally be taken as a natural result of her upbringing.

218. What the devil's going on here?: Daos' interpretation of what he has seen is predetermined both by what is later revealed as a naturally dour and suspicious character, and by the importance any family in antiquity, with a claim to respectability, attached to maintaining the reputation of its marriageable females totally without blemish. This explains the hostile reaction to Knemon, who has apparently been so irresponsible as

11

to lay his daughter open to being accosted by a total stranger, one who might well have designs on her that could ruin her marriage prospects. The audience knows, however, that the obstacle Knemon poses to the girl's marriage prospects is quite different, cf. 336ff.

230f. I see a carnival crowd: The cue for Daos' departure also serves as introduction to the entry of the chorus, whose arrival and presence are mentioned only at the end of the first Act in Menander's plays. Subsequent interventions by the chorus have no such reference, cf. *The Arbitration* 169ff., *The Rape of the Locks* 261ff., *The Shield* 246ff. For a while the action of the play now halts as a chorus of revellers enters with song and dance; that the lyrics they sing have not survived in the text is a strong indication that they constituted no more than an interlude unconnected with events in the play.

Act II

233. Gorgias: Further reducing the hiatus in the action caused by the intervention of the chorus is the impression now given of coming upon master and slave in the middle of their conversation (cf. 50). That Gorgias should regard Daos' failure to intervene in the incident between Sostratos and the girl as serious is made all the more pointed by the fact that Sostratos had actually walked past Daos as he exited to the audience's right in order to return home. In what follows, Gorgias soon begins to give evidence of possessing qualities that will allow him to fulfil his major function in the play: bridging the gulf between Sostratos and Knemon, town and country. So for instance, he echoes the rustic tendency to jump to conclusions (already seen in Daos' interpretation of Sostratos' motives), an understandable reaction in view of the source of his information. Like Knemon, he displays typical country prejudice against those raised in the easier environment of the city. Like Sostratos, however, he too considers that his servant does not always behave with the sense of responsibility expected of him.

247. Come on: i.e., towards Knemon's door. Daos' earlier complaint about the old man's carelessness over his daughter's security is now taken up by Gorgias, raising in the slave thoughts of a beating. In terms of logic, such fear is unjustified since Daos would hardly be punished by Knemon while his master looked on, but it serves both to reinforce the picture of the old man as totally unapproachable and to provide the cue for Gorgias' thumbnail sketch of his stepfather.

249. he'll string me up: For a beating, not by the neck.

256. Here comes that chap: As with the arrival of Pyrrhias on cue, this forms another instance of dramatic coincidence smoothing the flow of the action.

257. the smart city cloak: Like Knemon later at 754, Gorgias displays a distinct tendency to judge solely upon appearances. The contrast between the two young men is made all the more striking on a visual level by the fact that as a typical countryman Gorgias himself probably wore the *diphthera*, a leather jerkin mentioned in the context of the dream at 415.

259ff. Sostratos: The young man's monologue serves not only to explain his unexpected return to the stage at this point (cf. Arnott[1]), but also to introduce (by an element of foreshadowing) themes that only become relevant at a later stage: Sostratos' mother and the sacrifice, seeming irrelevancies at this point but destined actually to bring about the dénouement of the play (cf. Arnott[4] p. xxxvii).

261ff. she does this every day: This brief outline characterises her as a woman over-endowed with a superstitious sense of piety, but is also designed to show Sostratos once again as something of a spoilt adolescent, relieved not to have become caught up with the sacrifice, but peeved at having failed to secure the help he wanted just when he wanted it.

266. I've decided to cut out all this traipsing about: How are we to interpret this decision? It is tempting on the part of modern audiences to regard it as a welcome development in Sostratos' psychological make-up: a growth in maturity as a result of a series of frustrating disappointments – from a character who relies on others, to one prepared to act for himself. In the context of the ancient theatre, however, such an interpretation is unjustified, since to ancient thinking character was something established from birth, determined by nature not nurture. As a result, actual character development, beyond a realisation that previous actions were based on misapprehension, forms little part of dramatic productions, which in consequence were ethical, i.e., displayed already developed characters, rather than psychological. Within the context of the play too, Sostratos' resolve proves no more than a fleeting diversion in the overall picture; for once he is assured of Gorgias' support and friendship, he has no hesitation in using his new ally every bit as much as he earlier hoped to use Chaireas and Pyrrhias. Certainly Sostratos is willing to engage in manual labour in the vain hope of making a good impression on Knemon, but the initiative for this comes from elsewhere. What, then, does Sostratos' resolve here contribute to the action apart from restoring him to the scene? If anything, it reveals, I think, his continuing inability to accept the reality of Knemon's character despite the earlier indications accorded by his own and Pyrrhias' experience of the man, and the daughter's evident fear of him, an inability that underpins Sostratos' basic immaturity. At the same time it is clear that Menander actually uses

13

the audience's superior knowledge of Knemon to establish economically
(1) its appreciation of Sostratos' continuing misapprehension and (2) its
realisation that but for the intervention of Gorgias, Sostratos would in all
likelihood have met with the same fate as Pyrrhias earlier.

269ff.: The contrast between Sostratos and Gorgias, already established on a visual level, soon develops further in their contrasting patterns
of speech and thought. So for instance, Gorgias approaches the task of
warning off Sostratos in what Sandbach[1] aptly calls 'a comically formal,
almost pompous, style' involving long and meandering sentences. However, while his sentiments show him to have a well developed sense of
right and wrong (even if he does tend to simplify ethical and moral
questions into black and white), his phrasing indicates he has never been
accustomed to putting them into words. Hence, his argument develops
illogically and incoherently, as Sostratos' puzzled and non-committal
reaction in 288, with its use of the vague 'stepping out of line', indicates.
In addition, Gorgias' initial politeness and the element of pomposity in
his phrasing may well also be designed to indicate his unease at having to
approach an evidently sophisticated city-dweller, and his belief that such
a style is not only appropriate to the situation but will also impress.
Sostratos, in contrast, as we soon see, is very much more at ease: his
sentences flow into one another with unaffected facility (see further
Brenk p. 32f.).

274ff. The successful man...harming others: The contents of Gorgias' speech, that a person's fate will be in accordance with his deserts,
was something of a commonplace by Menander's day (see Arnott[6]
p. 224ff.), as Euripides fr. 1073 aptly shows 'A man who goes his way in
good fortune should not suppose that he will always have the same luck.
For the god – if one should use the word god – becomes tired of associating with the same people for ever. Mortals' prosperity is itself mortal:
those who are proud and trust in the future on the basis of the present find
in what happens to them that their future proves them wrong' (trans.
Handley[1]), cf. *Ion* 1621f., Dover p. 110ff.

282. credit: Commentators have been divided over interpretation of
this. Some, like Handley[1], have taken it in the sense of business credit (cf.
Demosthenes XXXVI, 44 'good credit is the greatest asset in business'),
though from the picture of Gorgias gradually built up, its application here
seems inappropriate. More likely, perhaps, he means no more than poverty borne with patience may win the poor man a better future at the
hands of Fate.

284. Let me put it this way: Clearly Gorgias realises that the extreme
generality of what he has said so far calls for something more relevant to
the situation.

288. stepping a bit out of line: The vagueness of the phrasing shows

Sostratos impressed by the tone of Gorgias' outpouring but at a loss as to what it has to do with him. It is this in turn that prompts Gorgias to come to the point, and we see immediately the contrast in Sostratos' reaction.

292. something that deserves the death-sentence: To the poor man with nothing to call his own but his family honour such a sentiment would not be out of place. Arnott[6] aptly points to the irony of Gorgias' accusation. In New Comedy, wealth and leisure almost invariably proved the prelude to illicit sexual activity by young men; yet Sostratos is portrayed throughout the play as virtuous and intent upon an honourable marriage.

297. he gets a lot of sympathy: That the plight of the poor man could readily arouse the sympathy of others was well recognised in antiquity, especially by those engaged in lawsuits, who were often found to plead poverty when the reverse was actually the case. That the opposite could also be true, however, is found stated in Menander's *The Farmer* fr.1.

298. personal insult: Gorgias uses here the Greek term *hybris*, a serious charge defined by Aristotle *Rhetoric* 1378 b 23 as 'so acting or speaking that the sufferer is disgraced, not in order to attain anything for oneself other than the performance of the act, but for pleasure...The cause of the pleasure for those who commit *hybris* is their belief that in maltreatment of others they are more fully displaying their superiority. For this reason the young and the wealthy are guilty of *hybris*, for they think that by committing it they are superior', cf. Philippides fr. 26 'for he who acts violently towards the weak man, Pamphilus, seems to be offering insult not injury.', MacDowell[1], Dover p. 54.

300. That's fair, sir: Daos' interjection before Sostratos begins his defence has been variously interpreted, since it is unclear in the Greek text to whom it is directed. Some, for instance, suggest it represents an attempt on the part of the slave to interrupt Sostratos and thus prevent him from giving any explanation of his behaviour. That this is unlikely, however, is well demonstrated by Sandbach[1] who argues that it is actually in Daos' interest that Sostratos should vindicate himself, since this would mitigate his earlier dereliction of duty in failing to intervene in the encounter with Knemon's daughter. If this is so, it represents the only occasion on which Daos shows any sympathy for Sostratos.

301ff.: In Sostratos' defence of his action the shortness and directness of his sentences reinforce the tone of sincerity in what he says.

307. I have a reasonable income: In view of what we learned from Pan in the Prologue (40) and later learn about Sostratos' father (773ff.) this would seem to be something of an understatement, a feature indeed of the young man's style of speech in general, but positively useful here in closing the gap between himself and Gorgias.

308. without a dowry: The usual form of marriage in ancient Greece was not founded upon a love match such as occurs in so many New Comedies, but upon a formal agreement between families which had important financial, as well as dynastic, implications. Within this, the dowry constituted the bride's contribution to her husband's household, a contribution which did not become his property but which he held in trust for any offspring, and which he was obliged to return in the event of divorce. This latter aspect, in fact, formed a significant safeguard against marrying simply for money or resorting too easily to divorce in the event of marital difficulties. Within New Comedy on the other hand, the willingness of a young man to forgo the dowry conventionally signified the sincerity of his feelings for the girl, cf. Diodorus Comicus fr. 3 'It's better to take a wife who's well brought up without a dowry than one badly brought up with money', Plautus' *The Pot of Gold* 478ff.

311. Pan...and the Nymphs: The irony of Sostratos' reference at exactly this moment cannot have been lost on the audience.

317. You've convinced me completely: Why has Menander allowed Gorgias' earlier hostility to Sostratos to be replaced by an offer of friendship with such speed that it appears unnatural? The answer lies perhaps in the dramatic needs of the moment. What, after all, would be gained from further suspicion? Instead, the ease with which Gorgias is won over may be seen as indicating the essential openness of his character, a pointed contrast to the other rustic males in the play, Daos and Knemon.

I'm on your side: lit. 'you have me as your friend'. It is in fact Gorgias' use of the word 'friend' which forms the cue for the next stage in Sostratos' plan (320), since friendship in its Greek context betokened not simply an emotional tie, but a recognition of mutual obligation to give help and support whenever needed, hence Sostratos' reciprocation at 615. That Gorgias himself recognises the implications of his statement is clear from his reaction to Sostratos' first hint of using his new-found friend (322f.): the doubt that he can provide any help at all, a doubt born of real understanding and thus a strong contrast to Chaireas' assurances.

333. with his daughter beside him: This is the only point of mitigation in Gorgias' depiction of Knemon as the totally antisocial type, but is intended by the playwright primarily to inspire Sostratos' determination to make a good impression on the old man.

344. There's no time: For love as the pursuit of the leisured see Theophrastus fr. 114: 'Asked what love is, he said "an affliction of a soul that has leisure"', Terence's *Self-Tormentor* 109 'Love arises from nothing other than excessive leisure', cf. the implications of Chaireas' question at 53.

347. it's in God's: Sostratos probably intends a reference here to Eros, the god of love, though the audience would again have seen in the statement an ironic pointer to the real source of Sostratos' affliction.

358f. No, but he'll soon be going out: How Gorgias knows Knemon is not in the fields invites rationalisation in terms of his seeing the old man leave after the incident with Pyrrhias. We have to admit, though, it is a question that occurs more readily to the reader than it probably did to the original audience, for whom the relentless progress of the drama, which allowed little time for reflection, invites acceptance of the situation presented and its underlying rationale. More important is the effect Gorgias' answer has on Sostratos: the hope that he will be able to see the girl again (note the contrast in 360 between Sostratos' eagerness and Gorgias' virtual indifference), which leads in turn to his willingness to engage in manual labour in order to impress Knemon. In the event, however, this becomes an instance of false foreshadowing, for Knemon never returns to the fields but is kept at home by the arrival of Sostratos' own mother and her entourage.

364. Are you going to stand there...we work away?: In the absence of any definite indication in the papyrus as to who speaks at this point, commentators have been divided between assigning the question to Gorgias or to Daos. In favour of the latter is the fact that the slave's name appears in the margin of the manuscript at 366 ('Because he'll throw...'). Furthermore, in the context of Daos' later statement at 371ff. ('What *I* want...') the suggestion that Sostratos engage in digging might well appear loaded with irony and designed specifically to lure the young man into a course of action meant to wear him down and thus end his attempt to win the girl. Similarly, attribution of the line to Gorgias has been seen as illogical since the whole tenor of his earlier suggestion at 350, that Sostratos go with him to the fields, seemed designed to show the impossibility of any approach to Knemon. The fact that the text at 350f. is fragmentary, however, makes certainty beyond reach, and attribution of 364 and 367ff. to Gorgias might well be taken as indicating his attempt to be helpful towards Sostratos, despite the poor chances of success he envisages, just as his mention of Sostratos' smart appearance at 364, echoing the sentiment of 357 ('elegant and idle'), makes the picture of hard work and an altered appearance essential to any progress.

375. mattock: The *dikella*, a two-pronged hoe designed to be used like a pick-axe and allow deeper working of land than could be achieved by a plough, or for use on rockier soils or in more confined spaces than the plough could work.

376. building up the wall: i.e., constructing a dry stone wall without the use of mortar, no less laborious than digging. Daos' ostensible generosity towards Sostratos is clearly designed with 372ff. in mind.

381ff.: Sostratos' departing speech emphasises the virtue of isolation – the fact that the girl will be ignorant of life's darker side and unencumbered by the faults men in antiquity commonly associated with women (cf. Sostratos' earlier criticism of his mother's superstitious tendencies). At the same time the description of Knemon as 'against all vice' forms an element in the gradual shift that takes place in characterising the old man – from total antisocial misanthropy to disgust at the hypocrisy of society. At what point does Gorgias leave the stage? Frost p. 47 argues for an exit at 381, so as to provide time for the actor to change into the costume of Getas in readiness for an entry from the opposite wing. Arnott[10], however, suggests that a simultaneous exit of Gorgias and Sostratos is both feasible and dramatically effective: (1) it solves the difficulty of Sostratos not knowing Gorgias' destination if they leave separately, and (2) it adds an extra dimension of comedy to Getas' slightly late arrival at 402.

390ff. Help!...on the job: These final sentences do much to lighten the scene in readiness for the entry of Sikon and Getas, and also to show Sostratos as capable of smiling at his own predicament, foreshadowing his later description of the effects of his labour.

393ff.: Like the earlier first entry of Daos, the first entries of the cook and slave form the bridge uniting Acts II and III. Similarly, the juxtaposition of Sostratos' complaint over the weight of the mattock and that from Sikon concerning the sheep mirrors a similar coincidence of complaints about Phyle and its inhabitants from them at 521f. Essentially, however, the introduction of Sikon and Getas here serves as an interlude of light comedy (cf. *The Shield* 216ff.) into which is injected foreshadowing for events that occur in Act III.

This sheep's a real beauty: Jokes about sacrificial animals, especially their quality, were commonplace in comedy, cf. Getas' description at 567, *The Girl from Samos* 399ff., or Euclio's complaint in Plautus' *The Pot of Gold* 561ff. Arnott[2] p. 15 points to a further linguistic pun introduced by Sikon in the very word for sheep in Greek, *probaton*, suggesting something that does go forward, and thus the complete opposite of the present case.

399. I'm the cook: Despite this self-identification Sikon's role would have been clear from the start as a result of the equipment he brought with him and the presence of the sheep. Cooks in antiquity, often hired for the occasion, were expected not only to prepare the meal but also to butcher the animal involved, hence the irony of Sikon being turned into mincemeat by his intended victim. For similar jokes see *The Girl from Samos* 283ff., Alexis fr.173 'Don't cut me up, cut up the meat instead', Anaxippus fr. 1 'It's me you'll cut to pieces not what we're supposed to sacrifice'.

401. Hey, Getas!: While identification of Sikon by profession could be left to external characteristics, the identification of Getas as the slave sought by Sostratos at 182 has to be achieved by use of his name at an

18

early stage in the scene. This then allows the injection of dramatic irony as the audience realises that he is not what Sostratos had claimed him to be, but that this is another instance of the young man's repeated misinterpretation of reality. At the same time it neatly restores to the action a character who previously received only a passing mention, just as the reference to the dream in 407, which reintroduces Sostratos' mother, reinforces the role of Pan in the action and demonstrates the relevance of the sacrifice mentioned earlier.

402. A four-donkey load: The image of the overburdened slave can be traced back to Xanthias at the beginning of Aristophanes' *Frogs*. The rugs are those upon which the sacrificial party will lie as they feast.

414. putting fetters on him: Probably the chains of love on the analogy of ancient depictions of Eros in chains, though according to Artemidorus II 37, to dream of Pan portended danger. To Keuls[1] on the other hand they represent Sostratos' willingness to engage in unaccustomed hard work i.e., symbolic slavery.

415. leather jacket: The *diphthera* probably worn also by Gorgias and symbolising the conversion of Sostratos into a quasi-countryman. There is no need of course to envisage the young man actually putting on such a garment in order to work in Gorgias' fields.

418. to make sure...ending: For analogous use of sacrifices to avert misfortune see Aeschylus' *Libation-Bearers* and *Persians*.

Act III

427. Lock the door: An unusual practice in daytime, since there was usually some servant or other available in a Greek household whose tasks included the admission of callers. Locking the door, therefore, is as much a sign of antisocial behaviour as it is when practised by Euclio in Plautus' *The Pot of Gold* 103f., cf. *The Ghost* 444. So far it seems that Sostratos' plan to meet Knemon will prove successful. Ironically, however, the intention is soon frustrated by the arrival on the scene of his own mother, whose voluble bossiness and attention to detail underpin Sostratos' earlier description of her and serve to arouse the old man's disgust.

430ff. Mother: The entry of Sostratos' mother and her party in front of Knemon increases visually the theme of intrusion upon his privacy. First there was the offstage approach of Pyrrhias, then the encounter on stage with Sostratos, and now a real crowd appears.

440. baskets, water: The former was used to hold food and offerings, or more specifically, the grains of barley sprinkled on the victim before it was sacrificed, the latter for ritual washing of the hands.

441. And what are *you* gaping at, hophead?: This is an exceptionally impertinent jibe from a slave to a free man, so much so that commentators have used the fact that its formulation is usually found in the context of social equals to suggest it is directed either by Getas at another slave, or by Sostratos' mother, impatient and stung by Getas' sarcasm, at Knemon. That Knemon at all events should be the object of the insult is clearly required by the dramatic situation (*pace* Frost p. 50); it is the final spur to the outpouring that comes next.

442. Damn and blast them!: In addition to confirming yet again Knemon's suspicious nature and extreme dislike of any who invade his exaggeratedly extensive personal space, the old man's parting speech introduces another aspect of his character: his belief that selfishness is the principal factor in determining the actions of others. As such, it constitutes an element of foreshadowing, like Sostratos' earlier description of him as a hater of evil, one that is only seen in its full significance after the accident down the well. That ancient sacrifices existed more for the benefit of the participants than for the gods was not a new idea, however. Menander treated it elsewhere in his play *Methe* or *Drunkenness* fr. 319 'So aren't our fortunes like our sacrifices? Whereas to the gods I bring a nice little sheep I bought for ten drachmas, the girl pipers, the perfume, harp-girls, Mendean and Thasian wine, the eels, cheese and honey cost almost a talent (6,000 drachmas)' cf. Plautus' *The Pot of Gold* 371ff. That the gods on the other hand had more regard for the character of the giver than the costliness of the offering was apparently maintained by Menander's teacher Theophrastus in his work *On Piety*, which in turn echoes Euripides fr. 327 'I often see poor men wiser than the rich, and in that they sacrifice small offerings to the gods, more pious than those who offer oxen'. We should, however, resist the temptation to see in Knemon's outburst serious social comment in tune with the attempt by Athens' pro-Macedonian ruler, Demetrius of Phaleron, to impose restrictions upon consumption, since Knemon is hardly a sympathetic advocate for such a proposition.

456. You've forgotten the *pot*: As well as providing a further aspect of his character, Knemon's outburst also allows time for discovering the lack of a suitable pot for cooking the sheep.

456-521: Menander deliberately introduces here an instance of scene repetition in the attempts of Getas and Sikon to borrow equipment, the one building upon the other towards a climax of comedy, cf. the repetition of Simiche's involvement with Getas (574ff.), then with Sikon (629ff.). In many ways the successive encounters of slave and cook with Knemon, in which they both come off worse, finds a mirror image in Act V when first Sikon and then Getas treat the old man to some of his own medicine. A similar use of parallel development occurs in *The Shield* with the reported deaths of Kleostratos and Chairestratos and the effect they have on Smikrines.

459. Door!: For New Comedy playwrights, attracting the attention of those inside a house provided a conventional opportunity for visual and spoken humour as the character involved employed patently exaggerated knocking and calling (cf. Plautus' *The Ghost* 898ff., Frost p. 9).

469. Is there any contract: The question is underpinned by Knemon's assumption that this could be the only reason anyone would choose to approach him. Instead, the bathos of Getas' real errand is emphasised by the repetition of 'pot', just as the incongruity of sacrificing bulls in the context of Knemon is pinpointed by Getas' reference to a snail.

477f. The women...No pot: Further evidence that Getas is anything but the sharp operator of Sostratos' imagination. At the first obstacle he retreats with the excuse that he has done all that was required of him.

481ff. Man-eating tigers: As with 442ff., Knemon's parting shot not only foreshadows subsequent developments, but satisfies the requirement of separating the departure of Getas and the unheralded arrival of Sikon, whose appearance on stage is readily accounted for by his continuing to address Getas inside the shrine. Like Sostratos with Pyrrhias, Sikon finds it impossible to accept the reality of Knemon until he experiences the old man himself; like Chaireas, his inflated view of his abilities, typical of stage cooks, invites disaster, an instance of Arnott's irony of failure (Arnott[2] p. 13f.).

492. borrow pots from them all: The propensity of cooks for stealing the equipment of others was a topic of humour in its own right, cf. *The Shield* 216ff. n.

500. You back again?: The question has caused commentators no small problem, but unnecessarily so. Taken at face value it suggests either that Knemon cannot tell Sikon and Getas apart, or that when Sikon enters, he is accompanied by Getas, to whom the question is addressed and the ironic description at 515 'There are ways and means of asking a favour...' may be attributed. According to some, indeed, it is in fact Getas who suffers the thrashing at the old man's hands while Sikon stands by attempting to maintain a diplomatic neutrality. That this is neither likely nor necessary, however, needs little demonstration. In the first place Knemon's question indicates not myopia but a tendency to equate all those who impinge on his privacy as one and the same, no more extreme a tendency than his earlier conversion of Pyrrhias into a horde. Similarly, Sikon's earlier pride in his skill invites such a fall, so that 515 becomes no more than an ironic admission of his failure.

505. a cook-pan: Why does Sikon ask for a different piece of equipment from that mentioned by Getas? Is its more imposing sound a mark of his continuing tendency to self-importance, or does it signify, as

Handley[1] hints, his belief that to ask for something not already refused displays greater politeness?

I haven't got one...: For a similar list of articles cf. Alexis fr. 174 'I don't happen to have either vinegar or dill or oregano or a fig leaf or olive oil or almonds or garlic or wine extract or leek or onion or fire or cummin or salt or eggs or wood or a kneading trough or a pan or rope...', Theophrastus *Characters* 10 'His wife is forbidden to lend either salt or a lamp-wick or cummin or oregano or barley grains or garlands or sacrificial cakes', Plautus' *The Pot of Gold* 90ff.

520. Be blowed to the locals!: lit. 'the people of Phyle', forming a verbal link between this scene and the next and providing the hint that for all its humour the scene with Getas and Sikon existed primarily to cover the time Sostratos was in the fields. Frost p. 53 suggests that Sikon's deliberative monologue may also be designed to smooth the transition to Sostratos' speech from the swiftness of what has just occurred.

522ff. Anyone who's short of trouble...: Sostratos' entry provides a telling visual contrast with his appearance when last seen. Now he is exhausted, sunburned, and perhaps minus his luxurious cloak. Totally unused to hard labour he has clearly failed to work himself into the task; instead he went at it full tilt from the beginning and as a result his exertions have taken a savage toll on both his energies and his muscles. One positive result, however, is the revelation of an ability to comment ironically on his painful experience, cf. the later description he gives of his role in the rescue of Knemon 666ff.

533. I started to straighten up: i.e., he attempted to arch his back in order to counteract the effect of constant forward bending. The only result of Sostratos' enthusiastic efforts, however, was increasing stiffness in the small of his back and pain across his shoulders (hence 'my neck' in 524) as he swung the mattock up above his head. The eventual effect is graphically described in 536f.: Sostratos' movements became like those of a well beam (shadoof), a device for raising water from shallow wells still used in many countries. It consists of a pivoted beam with a bucket attached by a rope at one end and a counterweight at the other. The operator hauls on the rope to make the bucket descend into the well while the counterweight then lifts it to the surface.

545. something draws me...to the place: Another gentle reminder of Pan's role in the situation. Only here at the end of the monologue does Sostratos in fact give some little information on his motive for returning.

552. And who are you?: Getas' failure to recognise his master at first is primarily explained by the effects of the smoke mentioned at 550, but may also be intended to give the audience some explicit reference to the change in Sostratos' appearance, similar to Knemon's remarks at 754. At this point further strands in the overall plot are brought into contact: the love plot and the sacrifice.

558ff. I'll go...to join us: Menander injects another indication that Sostratos remains essentially parasitic on the efforts and arrangements of others. Earlier he had been happy not to become involved in the sacrifice, regarding it as a nuisance that robbed him of Getas' services; now he is quite prepared to make use of it for his own purposes – further bolstering his new-found friendship – but with the additional calculation that it will extend Gorgias' obligation to offer help in the future.

563ff. Oh?...: Like his reaction at 425f., Getas' words are full of irony and sarcasm. Already he has shown himself singularly unimpressed by the amount of work the sacrifice is causing him in coming to the shrine at all and the need to get things ready inside; now Sostratos' intention of inviting additional guests further reduces his chances of getting much of a share in the festivities.

570. a pinch of cooking salt: Like the refusal to give a thirsty traveller water, the denial of salt, one of life's essentials in a hot climate, was a proverbial mark of miserliness and unsocial behaviour.

572. Pan: A further reminder of the god, and it may be significant that it comes from Sostratos himself just before the series of events leading directly to Knemon's escapade down the well.

574. Oh calamity...: Despite the continued presence of Getas on stage it is clear that Simiche's outpouring of panic is not directed at him. Its narrative content indeed, revealing what she herself knows only too well, shows the essentially artificial nature of the stage monologue, designed as it is simply to keep the audience informed of developments while maintaining a veneer of dramatic illusion. Through all of it, indeed, Getas' role is to lighten by his asides and comments what might otherwise have been a scene of some pathos. With Simiche's outpouring comes the second of those references to the well that cause a character to exit from Knemon's house (cf. 189ff., 620ff.). As Frost p. 54 observes, all have tragic overtones, though the present instance is clearly designed to produce a comic effect.

579f. I tied the mattock...rope: The description is a further indication of Knemon's self-imposed frugality (cf. 327f. where Gorgias had indicated the old man's resources were not meagre), matching his mania for self-reliance. The latter in fact explains his reaction to Simiche's suggestion that they call upon Daos for help (594), which mirrors in turn his insistence upon working the land alone and his tendency to exaggerate – interpreting the loss of the mattock as general ruin (595).

597. Oh dear...not a soul to help: How can Knemon be justified in bewailing his isolation when it is this he has striven to maintain all along? As a result of the fragmentary nature of the text here some commentators have suggested that the reference to isolation may signify no more than the loss of the mattock, but if so, Knemon has chosen uncharacterisically vivid language with which to express himself. Is it perhaps an early piece of foreshadowing for his later realisation (717) that he can no longer maintain total independence, a passing pang of regret that Getas' offer of help immediately sweeps aside?

604. That's your genuine Attic farmer: A further softening of the picture of Knemon as totally unsympathetic, with which the play opened. Getas' description, with its almost sentimental appeal, portrays Knemon as something of a paradigm of the poor farmer whose character is determined by the hard life imposed on him by nature.

611f. I simply won't take no for an answer: In addition to bridging the gap between Acts and ensuring that Sostratos and Gorgias are near at hand in readiness for the rescue, the entry of the pair also serves to characterise both Gorgias, for all his helpfulness, as the shy countryman (something we see again later), and Sostratos as still expecting that others will acquiesce in what he wants.

615. your friend I've been...before we met: This forms a specious factor in Sostratos' attempts to persuade Gorgias to join in the festivities, but is not totally untrue in so far as Sostratos interprets his love for Knemon's daughter as sufficient to require of him friendly, if calculated, relations with all the girl's family, even if such relations are more usually associated with the period after a marriage.

617f. Don't...leave my mother alone in the house: Though Gorgias' mother has in fact been alone since Daos left at 206, the insertion serves:

1) to repeat the concern Gorgias feels for his family, demonstrated earlier in the context of his step-sister at the beginning of Act II, and perhaps to introduce a subtle if unspoken distinction in his thinking between leaving his mother when work calls and leaving her alone simply in order to indulge in personal pleasure;

2) to ensure that Daos is not available to participate in the rescue;

3) to show Gorgias has not fallen so far under the spell of Sostratos that he gives way to the latter's every command – the running of his household is still his own responsibility and countermanding Sostratos' orders to Daos, like his determination not to remain in the shrine for long, signifies that Gorgias still has a mind of his own.

Act IV

620ff. Simiche: In many respects the scene mirrors that in Act III when Simiche dropped the mattock down the well. There, it was Getas who provided the stage-audience for her terror, now it is the cook.

Earlier, Knemon had threatened to lower her into the well to retrieve the mattock and bucket; now she is urged to reverse roles and to drop something heavy on to Knemon. More importantly, however, Sikon's interjections direct the audience's reaction to the event away from its tragic potential, and ensure that once the rescue party has left, the audience is not faced with an empty stage.

623. You insult us: Like Knemon earlier, Sikon generalises from the specific beating given him by one crusty old man to his whole family.

639ff. There *is* a God…: Sikon prefaces his main task in the monologue – envisaging the process of rescue – with an instance of typical cook's boastfulness and self-importance which, like his earlier interjections, steers the scene away from possible gloom. Thus, after heightening suspense by repeating verbatim the girl's cries inside, Sikon diverts attention to what he sees as the positive effects of Knemon's discomfiture for himself and others.

647. but you can…way you like: The reference serves as a fleeting reminder of the quarrelling between caterers that was something of a comic cliché, cf. the end of *The Shield* Act I, Handley[1] *ad loc.*

666. Sostratos: While the entry of Sostratos signals the transition from imagined to real events, Menander continues the suspense already built up by Sikon by delaying to the very end of the opening sentence the true extent of Knemon's troubles: 'half-drowned', thereby mirroring in fact the cook's own use of the device in 661f.: 'Pray that the old man's rescue may be – bungled…'. With the relief of tension thus effected, the scene is then directed even closer to comedy through Sostratos' account of events in a style that is at once engagingly self-deprecating but typically self-centred.

670. Gorgias jumped straight down into the well: M. Anderson p.207 argues that Gorgias is given the major part in the rescue so that he can refute Knemon's philosophy of life all the more effectively, since it is Gorgias who actually has least reason to help – as the old man himself is later to recognise, 722ff. At the same time, however, we need to recognise the incongruity that would have arisen if Sostratos had done more than the bare and ineffectual minimum he does. Only now in fact, after numerous attempts in the past to profit from the exertions of others, has he found a helper who lives up to expectations.

683. Atlas: A Titan condemned forever to hold up the heavens; hence, while Sostratos was supposed to haul Knemon out of the well by means of a rope, Gorgias supported the old man from below and thus prevented the worst effects of Sostratos' lapses.

690: Apart from the reference to wheels at 758, and Knemon's request to be raised at 701 and lowered at 740 (which suggests he was initially lying down), the means by which the old man is brought out of his house is not mentioned in the text, and commentators have varied greatly in their restoration of stage action at this point, often as a result of their insistence upon maintaining an excessive degree of strict logicality in the scene. The most likely suggestions include use of either a wheeled couch, as in the translation, or the ekkyklema, a movable platform used to bring onto the stage ostensibly indoor scenes or tableaux. In favour of the latter, it may be argued that there is no real reason for bringing Knemon outside at all, so that the ekkyklema maintains the technical fiction of an indoor scene, though this does involve Knemon 'inside' interacting with Sostratos outside. The regularity with which indoor events are brought out into the open in New Comedy, however, easily disposes of the need for recourse to specific stage machinery, while the only real objection to the use of a wheeled couch – that it is an incongrous piece of furniture in the context of Knemon's household – is only valid if New Comedy was at all concerned to preserve such scrupulous logic.

693. Knemon...any of you again: The old man's belief that he is seriously injured is an essential prerequisite for the arrangements he is soon to make for disposing of both his farm and responsibility for his daughter. Only in this way, in fact, can Sostratos win the girl and Gorgias gain the reward he deserves.

698. Ask your mother to come: Presumably so that she can be a witness to the arrangements Knemon wishes to make.

710ff.: Knemon's defence of his lifestyle, delivered in longer verse lines (trochaic tetrameters) than those used in the dialogue so far, reveals the reality of what has so far only been hinted at in references from others (cf. Goldberg[2] p. 86). His unsociability is now shown to be not a self-generated phenomenon of his psychology, but symptomatic of a deliberate and conscious intellectual choice on his part, made as a result of his reaction to the selfishness he believed to underlie the behaviour of others. This led to his rejection of interaction with his fellow men and to the obsession with self-suffiency he has long shown (cf. 594ff.). Now, however, the one person who has least cause to react favourably to him, Gorgias, has demonstrated beyond doubt that the possibility of disinterested kindness does exist and deserves to be rewarded (cf. *The Farmer* 55ff.). That Knemon does not, however, order the logic of his statements with any degree of coherence has proved troublesome, to the extent that some have wrongly been tempted to see as entirely separate factors Knemon's recognition that his days of self-sufficiency are over and his disgust at what he interpreted as selfishness in others (cf. Arnott[11] p. 31). True, there is no logical connection between 'You always need to have...to help you' and 'When I saw how people lived', but their positioning side by side is enough to connect them into a single, if somewhat disorganised, thought-pattern.

714. self-sufficient: Though Knemon's insistence upon self-reliance has manifested itself in antisocial behaviour, this, like so much else in his make-up, is not a totally negative factor. Self-sufficiency was in fact an ideal state in Greek thought as Aristotle *Nichomachean Ethics* 1177 a 28ff. makes clear: 'And the self-sufficiency that is spoken of must belong to the contemplative activity. For while a philosopher, as well as a just man or one possessing any other virtue, needs the necessaries of life, when they are sufficiently equipped with things of that sort the just man needs people towards whom and with whom he shall act justly, and the temperate man, the brave man, and each of the others is in the same case, but the philosopher, even when by himself, can contemplate truth, and the better the wiser he is; he can perhaps do so better if he has fellow workers, but still he is the most self-sufficient' (trans. Ross).

731. I'm adopting you as my son: A necessary prerequisite to arranging the marriage of the daughter. Knemon will himself soon declare his inability to find a husband for her he would approve of (734). By adopting Gorgias therefore, who thus becomes heir to both the estate and the role of guardian to the girl, Knemon ensures that his death, which he regards as imminent, does not leave her in the position of a fatherless heiress and faced by the same problems as confront Kleostratos' sister in *The Shield*. In other circumstances a man with only female offspring would adopt a son and then marry his daughter to him, something, however, precluded in the present case by the particular blood relationship of Gorgias and the girl as offspring of the same mother.

735. leave me to live my own life: Why does Menander not parallel Knemon's acceptance that he can no longer be self-sufficient with a reform of his social behaviour? The answer perhaps lies in:

1) the fact that his earlier antisocial actions have been shown to spring from a positive aspect of his personality as a 'hater of evil', which in turn removes the necessity for total reform;

2) the tendency of the ancients to regard character as fixed rather than something liable to undergo modification;

3) the inconsistency of having someone who has so far been painted in such extreme colours undergo a complete transformation.

In fact, by giving up all responsibilities Knemon chooses to withdraw even further from society and it is only the efforts of Sikon and Getas in Act V that induce him to reverse the process, albeit grudgingly, a powerful indicator that Knemon continues to lie at the heart of the action to the very end of the play.

749. if you agree: Though Knemon has by now abrogated all responsibility for himself or his family, it is essential that at least some form of contact be made between future father-in-law and son-in-law; hence Gorgias' final attempt to bring the two together and involve the old man in the choice of Sostratos as husband for the girl. In some respects Knemon's reluctance here, gradually worn down as it is, foreshadows developments in the final Act, where he is cajoled into joining the celebrations of a marriage he probably now agrees to.

754. He's certainly been in the sun: Like Gorgias when he first saw Sostratos, Knemon's reaction is governed by external factors, though it is only the mention that Sostratos took part in the rescue (753) that induces the old man to give him any consideration at all. Ironically, however, the evident failure of Sostratos' aim in agreeing to work on Gorgias' land – to attract the attention of Knemon – now leads to precisely the result earlier hoped for as the old man is induced to accept a fiction he himself introduces (cf. 367ff.).

754f. Yes, and a good one...all day: How are we to interpret Gorgias' statements here? On one level his assertions are plainly false; for though Sostratos has been willing to engage in manual labour, his whole background is one that suggests he would indeed 'stroll idly around all day', a description that Gorgias himself applied at 357: 'looking elegant and idle'. On one level, therefore, Gorgias seems to engage in deliberate deception of his step-father, something totally out of keeping with the honest and forthright character established in the rest of the play, and suggestive of a dramatic lapse on the playwright's part (cf. Arnott[11] p. 29ff.). On the other hand, it might not be unjustified to see the statement as delivered 'tongue-in-cheek', with Gorgias ready to concur in a fiction not of his own making, and prepared to accept the irony of Knemon's observation for the sake of a marriage he had earlier deemed impossible, involving, as he soon openly recognises, 764ff., someone who has, on one occasion at least, taken on the role of a farmer.

760. consult your family: It was no less necessary for Sostratos to gain the consent of his own father for the marriage than that of the girl's legal guardian. The approaching wedding, for all that it was and still is a love-match (at least from Sostratos' viewpoint), remains essentially an agreement between families, hence the necessity of introducing Kallipides.

769f. A man like that...with a good grace: Gorgias' observation here echoes his complaint at 271ff.

774. Is Kallipides your father?: Gorgias' instant recognition of Kallipides, while being ignorant of his son, was motivated from the start by Pan's description of Sostratos as essentially a townsman. Kallipides himself adds nothing to the dramatic action here at the end of Act IV; instead, he forms the bridge with Act V, where his role is more clearly defined, and reduces the pace of the Act before its end.

Act V

The fact that the end of Act IV saw to all intents and purposes the resolution of Sostratos' love intrigue, which has so far been the motivating force of the action, but not the end of the play, is itself a strong indication of the plot's multiple facets. True, Menander has brought to a successful conclusion the process initiated by Pan and described in the prologue, but it is a process that has engendered developments of its own which are still incomplete. For instance, there is the need (1) to reward Gorgias for the help he has given his new-found friend; and (2) to draw Knemon, for all his increased isolation, into the festivities of the betrothal. In order to achieve the latter with some degree of plausibility, Menander is able to develop consequences resulting from the old man's earlier rough treatment of cook and slave in line with the atmosphere of pantomime slapstick and unreality which characterises the final Act of other New Comedy plays. He thus avoids the logical problem of having to induce someone well established as unapproachable and beyond persuasion into a course of action clearly unthinkable in other circumstances. The first loose end, on the other hand, requires the introduction of altogether fresh developments.

784. You're not doing all that I wanted, Father: The Act opens with a fleeting instance of false preparation. When last seen Sostratos' task was to win over his father to the idea of a marriage with Knemon's daughter. Now at the very beginning of the Act the playwright momentarily raises the prospect of an obstacle to it, an apparent reference to something known, before its conversion to something completely new, the projected betrothal of Gorgias to Sostratos' sister, which is not actually mentioned till 794 when Sostratos' argument reveals the two events as inextricably entwined within his mind.

797. You're talking about money, a very unstable substance: In the context of a century when fortunes were a prey to political upheavals, Sostratos' advice makes remarkable sense, more so in fact than his character warrants. His speech indeed echoes to no small degree the basis of Gorgias' own advice at 274ff., and it is clearly designed to counter what New Comedy often portrayed as a besetting sin of old age – the preoccupation with money (cf. Terence *The Brothers* 833ff.) – with equally commonplace sentiments on the transience of wealth, cf. *The Farmer* fr. 2, Euripides' *Phoenissae* 555ff. 'Mortals hold their possessions not as private goods, but rather we have charge of things that are the gods'.

Whenever they wish, they take them back again', Alexis fr. 281 'Of all good things count wealth the least; for it is the most insecure of all the things we possess' (see further Dover p. 277).

811f. A real friend is much better value: The idea is based, of course, on that of mutual obligation between friends, a concept that Kallipides' reaction shows he fully endorses, though we may also recognise that his continued resistance to the idea of a dual marriage-tie would serve no dramatic purpose at this point: resistance when it comes appears from quite an unexpected quarter.

821. I heard all your conversation: A technical use of the New Comedy convention of eavesdropping which allows Gorgias to become directly involved in the situation without the need for repetition of detail from Sostratos. Note the unmotivated entry of Gorgias, cf. *The Shield* 399ff., Frost p. 32.

828f. But for me...thank you, but – : This is a telling reaction from Gorgias since it reveals that Sostratos' character has changed little in the course of the play: he still remains the young man who blithely organises others' lives without considering their own wishes or consulting them. Similarly, it restates the earlier portrayal of Gorgias as someone capable of resisting his friend's tendency to do this (617f.), and with clearly greater effect than Kallipides was able to manage.

830. the proceeds of other people's hard work: Gorgias' resistance to the offer of a life of ease and his insistence upon making a living by his own efforts, echoes, if not in quite such an extreme form, Knemon's earlier obsession with self-reliance. At the same time the reference to the financial side of any marriage alliance with Kallipides' family raises the natural but as yet unspecified topic of the dowry that would come with Sostratos' sister. As Gorgias soon makes clear, his objection is born not of feelings of inferiority in either character or social standing, but is based simply on the discrepancy of wealth between the two families, cf. Menander fr. 583 'When someone who is poor chooses to marry and gains wealth as well as a wife, he hands over himself rather than receives her', Plautus' *The Pot of Gold* 474ff.

839. I'd be doubly deficient: Just as earlier Kallipides was won over to Sostratos' proposal with remarkable ease and speed, so now the speed with which Gorgias gives in to his future father-in-law's arguments betokens not so much the insincerity of his earlier protestations, nor weakness in the playwright's dramatic technique, but the fact that further resistance would add nothing to the situation. Significantly, it is Kallipides, who had earlier shown resistance to the idea of Gorgias as a son-in-law, who now wins over the young man. In this way he confirms his own expression of sincerity in 819, and becomes a fitting advocate for similar acceptance of the proposed marriage on the part of Gorgias. So it is that Menander brings to a close the tension between town and country, rich and poor, that has run through the play.

844. £30,000: lit. 3 talents (18,000 drachmas). Though probably an exaggeration in comparison with real life (*pace* Webster[2] p. 25f.), the size of dowries in New Comedy generally reflected the wealth of those who offer them; hence the affluent Kallipides provides three times the sum available to Gorgias, whose £10,000 (1 talent) constitutes half the value of Knemon's farm (see 327f., 738).

850. We'll all stay: Once again Sostratos insists on imposing his own timetable and plans upon the rest of the party.

855ff. We must have…: Technically, the continued presence of Sostratos and Kallipides fills the time for Gorgias to arrange the transfer of his household to the shrine, while also allowing for the introduction of an inconsequential and well-worn jibe at the alcoholic tendencies of women, cf. Alexis fr. 167 'Women have enough if there's enough to drink', Antiphanes fr. 56 'Very unfortunate is the man who marries a wife, except among the Scythians, where the vine doesn't grow'. Similarly, the reference to the men doing 'the night work' could be guaranteed to raise a smile with its sexual innuendo.

864. I've achieved a marriage: The claim introduces an attractive instance of irony since it is patently clear that Sostratos has contributed less to the achievement of his marriage than virtually any other character in the play. As MacCary[2] p. 305 observes, 'Sostratos has been literally a spectator at the arrangement of his own future'. Despite this, however, Sostratos' continued ignorance of his own contribution (or lack of it) remains one of his most attractive characteristics.

869. so that he could be absolutely on his own: Knemon's wish to dispense with Simiche too not only motivates her inclusion in the festivities, despite the omission of any reference to her from Sostratos at 847ff., but more importantly draws attention to the total solitude of the old man. This is further emphasised when she appears in person, and is of course necessary for the final events of the play, cf. 877 'Something awful will happen to you'. In this way Menander disguises necessity by a typical instance of naturalistic forward-planning.

871f. I'm shy with women in the same – : Just before Gorgias and Sostratos disappear for the last time Menander inserts a final instance of contrast between the two. Though Gorgias has often shown himself capable enough of defending his own authority and independence against encroachment by his new friend, he remains essentially a countryman unused to society in general and unsure of how to react to virtual strangers, one of whom, we may note, is his future bride. Sostratos on the other hand remains ever the optimist, confident and at ease in company.

880. what do you mean by fluting at me: The intervention of music at this point, matched by a change of metre to iambic tetrameters, marks a shift away from both the normal dialogue format thus far used in the Act and the quasi-reality of events portrayed. In their place we find the introduction of an atmosphere imbued with the bustle and knock-about humour of fantasy as Getas and Sikon turn the tables on Knemon, and by cajoling (cruel were it not for the comedy of the scene) induce him to take part in the festivities, cf. W.S. Anderson[2] p. 161ff. The instrument referred to here is a pipe which used a double reed for the production of its sound, rather like a modern oboe. Those illustrated in the context of the theatre appear to have been about 14 inches long and in many cases had twin pipes joined to a single mouthpiece which were played simultaneously with both hands.

891. your recent – er – experience?: The force of Sikon's reply to Getas' question suggests he sees in the ostensibly innocuous vocabulary the suggestion of buggery.

898. suppose we haul him out first: Once again Menander sidesteps an incongruity of his own making: the presentation on stage of a scene which Knemon's health and immobility suggest would be more naturalistically depicted indoors. Rather than fudge the issue the playwright meets it head-on by converting the necessity of an outdoor staging into a dramatic virtue, presenting Getas' suggestion as an improvement on Sikon's original intention, and then allowing the slave to overcome the cook's subsequent qualms about being caught in the act.

907. Hang on a minute: Stage action at this point and the means by which Knemon is brought out of his house have been much disputed: whether, for instance, both characters enter in order to bring him out or only one enters, and the means by which the old man is actually brought onto the stage.

909. Over to the right: i.e., the centre of the stage, in front of Pan's shrine, where the dramatic situation demands the scene be played, despite Sikon's earlier concern not to attract Gorgias' attention. Since it was Sikon who initiated the idea of making demands on the old man (896), it is perhaps more logical to have him begin the coming action rather than Getas, as proposed by some editors who prefer to maintain symmetry with Act III. The papyrus itself gives no indication of detailed attribution of parts here, but the items sought, cooking pans etc. by one, rugs etc. by the other, again suggest the order of approach to Knemon is first Sikon then Getas.

913. Who's this?: Sikon's supposed failure to have noticed Knemon lying outside is, of course, all part of the fantastic pretence the two engage in: an approach to the door with apparently thunderous knocking (922) followed by exaggerated demands made to Knemon himself, all in an atmosphere of pantomime 'reality' that culminates in Sikon's description of the party inside, its preliminaries (936ff.), and a fanciful display of metaphor and imagery (946ff.) – 'venerable old vintage' (wine), 'Naiads' rill' (water) – which mirrors his style of speech throughout the play.

956. Shall we take you to the party, then?: At last the real purpose of the scene is revealed: behind the theme of vengeance for Knemon's earlier rough treatment of the two lies the dramatic need to dispose of the last loose end: Knemon's refusal to join the party. Since his desire for isolation has consistently been shown to have a positive aspect to it, it would be inconceivable to portray him giving this up voluntarily; hence compliance comes only as a preferable course to continued harassment.

959ff. Hooray: With the action virtually complete, the atmosphere, and with it the metre, returns to that of normal dialogue for the finale. This includes the traditional procession off stage – complete with torches and garlands – and an appeal to the goddess Victory and the audience for favour, something already present in the plays of Aristophanes: *Acharnians* 1227ff., *Birds* 1763ff., *Ecclesiazusae* 1179ff., cf. Menander's *The Girl from Samos*. Since Getas is required to address the audience in the closing lines, his role as support for Knemon is taken over by the slave Donax, summoned from inside.

964. bring us garlands: The reference is important evidence for the use of extras or mutes in the plays. As Frost p. 3ff. demonstrates, these can range from pure extras, as here, to specific characters, such as Syros' wife in *The Arbitration*, whose function is to hold the baby during the arbitration scene.

The Girl from Samos
or The Marriage Connection

Act I

In contrast to *Old Cantankerous*, information about the dramatic antecedents of *The Girl from Samos* and its major characters is provided not by a god but by one of the individuals intimately involved in the action. On a technical level, the change is hardly felt; it is the natural outcome of developing a plot that does not hinge upon some factor unknown to all the characters portrayed. As Bain[1] p. 187f. observes, the shift from divine to human exposition results at most in the failure of Moschion to set the scene by the blatant means Pan uses in *Old Cantankerous*, or (so far as we can tell in the absence of the opening lines), to step outside his role and specifically refer to the audience as Misapprehension does in *The Rape of the Locks*. In dramatic terms, on the other hand, Menander's use of Moschion as quasi-prologue speaker has important repercussions for the audience's reaction to the details he provides; for while his role suggests that element of objectivity we expect from a divinity – an expectation the playwright does nothing to dispel – it becomes clear as the action progresses that much of what the young man reveals as fact is in truth highly subjective, cf. Brenk p. 35 ff.

The result is the creation of a wide-ranging tension between perception and reality, between expected and actual behaviour, which entertains by the repeated portrayal of good intentions frustrated by weaknesses of character. It is this indeed which largely allows the play to extend to five Acts, since in many respects the underlying theme of the drama, a marriage that everyone wants and is constantly striving to bring about, holds little ostensible promise for developing New Comedy's essential characteristic: overcoming the obstacles that stand in the way of the play's ultimate goal. In this respect too, comparison with plays like *Old Cantankerous* or *The Shield* reveals a shift in dramatic technique; for whereas in those plays the obstacle involved is externalised in the figures of Knemon and Smikrines, that in *The Girl from Samos* is internalised, portrayed in the more abstract and arguably more sophisticated guise of inter-relationships between individuals.

3. I *did* do wrong: Insertion of the admission so close to the play's opening not only whets the audience's appetite to learn the substance behind it, but also accounts for Moschion's clearly emotional state and thus provides the pretext for revelation of further details.

11. 'one of the crowd': The meaning of the phrase is uncertain and complicated by damage to the text. To some it marks a vague reference to the supposedly common position of all young men before they came of age, to others an attempt on Moschion's part to gloss over the real position of privilege he has enjoyed and which he details in 13ff., to others still an early instance of that modesty which manifests itself positively in shame for his behaviour towards Plangon, and negatively in his later failure to reveal the truth to his father.

12. I certainly wasn't...in my mouth: The fragmentary text (lit. 'even more lowly') prevents certainty of interpretation, but the statement may be a veiled reference to Moschion's adoptive status, perhaps first mentioned in the play's lost opening and confirmed by 346f. Why though has Menander chosen to make Moschion an adopted son rather than Demeas' true offspring? A partial explanation may lie in the greater ease of representing Demeas' liaison with Chrysis if he were a bachelor rather than a widower, who might be expected to take a second wife rather than a mistress. More important, however, are the implications of adoption on the relationship between father and son. In the case of a blood-tie the connection is inescapable; a father might react to his son's misbehaviour with any degree of anger, as Menedemus does in Terence's *The Self-Tormentor* or Demea does in *The Brothers* – both plays derived from Menandrean originals – and yet preserve intact the bond that links them together. In the case of an adoptive son the bond is nowhere as strong or inescapable. The result for Moschion and Demeas, therefore, is a relationship in which each is careful to consider the interests of the other, even on occasion at considerable personal cost. It helps to explain, for instance, Demeas' initial embarrassment at revealing his affair with a mistress (27), his readiness to expel Chrysis from his home rather than accept even the possibility of any wrong-doing by his son (328ff.), and his desire to protect Moschion's reputation even when Moschion himself seems intent upon destroying it (465f., 470f.). Such regard emerges too on the other side in the help given to Demeas when establishing Chrysis as his mistress and Moschion's claim to have repaid a generous upbringing with proper behaviour (18). Where the two differ, is in their reaction to the belief that the other has let him down: Demeas, that Moschion has had an affair with Chrysis, Moschion, that Demeas could think him capable of such an act (see further 695f. n.).

13. I backed a dramatic production: lit. 'acted as choregos', a position that required considerable financial outlay and, like that of cavalry officer, had at one time been restricted to older men.

18. I behaved myself: The Greek is later echoed by Demeas at 273 'he's always been a good boy' and at 344 'always been well-behaved'. The implication of Moschion's claim is that he did not become a prey to *hybris* (cf. *Old Cantankerous* 298 n.), hence his contributions to charity and help to friends in need, similarly mentioned at *Old Cantankerous* 807f. Within the claim, however, there is also an element of irony since, as we soon learn, this well behaved young man is also a rapist.

21. Samos: An island off the coast of Asia Minor which had long been subject to Athens and its inhabitants dispossessed of their land by Athenian settlers. In the Greek text Moschion refers to Chrysis' relationship to Demeas as that of a *hetaira* (mistress, lit. 'female companion'), whose attractions were basically sexual. Once installed in Demeas' house, however, Chrysis takes on many of the characteristics of more permanent concubine (*pallake*) status, someone who might act as housekeeper, until with the outburst at 130 the *hetaira* position resurfaces, a reaction perhaps to the sense of trust the old man feels has been betrayed.

22. it could happen to anyone: The manner in which Moschion reveals his father's affair is highly suggestive. His description, for instance, implies an element of worldly wisdom and maturity but is later belied in Act V by his own petulant desire for vengeance. At the same time it clearly contains an element of condescension – that Moschion knew what was best for his father and helped him to achieve it – reinforced by the matter-of-fact style adopted and the evident pride felt at discovering the affair despite Demeas' efforts to keep it secret, lit. ' He kept it quiet; he felt embarrassed. *I* found out about it for all his precautions and I reckoned…'. Again, however, the essential subjectivity of the information given becomes apparent when, for all Moschion's ability to organise other people's lives, the need to reveal his own relationship with Plangon reduces him to helplessness (63ff.). Throughout this whole section of the monologue, in fact, it becomes clear that Moschion is totally unable to view personal relationships except by reference to himself.

23. being a bit embarrassed: Moschion applies to Demeas the same Greek word (repeated in 27 'He felt a bit awkward') as he later applies to himself at 47f. 'I'm ashamed' and 67 'It's too embarrassing', thereby underlining the bond between father and son through the very language he employs. In many ways too Demeas' embarrassment reverses the New Comedy norm in which it was the young man who found himself unable to reveal the existence of a mistress (see further Grant p. 177ff.).

37f. they'd visit us, too: The close ties of friendship between the families described at this early stage of the action neatly establish how Plangon came to be in Demeas' house on the night of the rape and avoid the need for any later explanation of why Demeas and Nikeratos are on a joint business venture despite the apparent disparity in their fortunes.

49. The girl got pregnant: Since it was inconceivable that a respectable girl in antiquity would voluntarily enter into a pre-marital sexual relationship, rape became the only means of introducing the theme of unscheduled pregnancies into plays, whether tragic, as in Euripides' *Ion*, or comic, as in Menander's *The Arbitration* or Plautus' *The Pot of Gold*. In New Comedy, such acts of rape might be mitigated in part by reference to the effects of alcohol, though clearly this is not the case with Moschion – if anything, it is the women, 'making a night of it' (46), who may have been drunk. Instead, by way of mitigation Menander is careful to emphasise Moschion's regret and his desire to rectify the wrong by admitting responsibility and a promise of marriage. At this early stage in the play we can only take the statements at face value, though as Goldberg[2] p. 95 observes, the fact that Parmenon has to remind him of his obligations at 63-9 calls the depth of his earnestness into question when it apparently conflicts with the father–son tie.

56. Chrysis...had her baby too: The most frequently adopted restoration of the damaged text at this point, since such a birth followed by the infant's early death (cf. *The Arbitration* 268) would readily explain Chrysis' ability to pose as the mother of Plangon's baby even to the extent of feeding it. Many commentators, however, have found such a scenario impossible to accept, and have argued instead:

1) The reference to Chrysis nursing the child at 266 need not imply she was actually feeding it, merely that she was comforting it.

2) The inability of Chrysis to feed the child would explain why Plangon was discovered performing this function at 535.

3) This would also rescue Chrysis from the imputation of self-interest: of having borne a child, no matter what its fate, without the apparent knowledge, and certainly without the permission, of the lover on whom she depends, in an effort to strengthen the bond that tied him to her.

To each of these points, however, is an equally possible counter-argument:

1) The parallel phrasing used at 266 and 535 suggests a similarly parallel act, one bolstered in Chrysis' case by the implications, if not the actual wording, of 77ff: 'Do we let Chrysis here go on *nursing* it...?'. Significantly too, nothing subsequently occurs to undermine Demeas' interpretation of seeing Chrysis with the baby at her breast, and for both women to be seen feeding the child allows a telling contrast of reaction between the two old men: Demeas self-controlled yet mistaken over the

mother's identity, Nikeratos outraged at what he has seen yet correct in his interpretation.

2) Plangon's feeding of the child at 535 is inserted not to indicate that only she is capable of such an act, but for the effect it has on Nikeratos. Furthermore, the presence of the baby in Nikeratos' house by that point makes it natural that its real mother should take her turn in suckling it.

3) Nowhere in the extant text is there any suggestion that Chrysis' actions are motivated by self-interest. Instead, the loyalty and attachment to the baby she displays, despite considerable problems for herself and the opportunity to give the child up at 374, suggest that thoughts of personal advantage never arise (cf. West). Yet does the question of Chrysis' having had a baby exist as an isolated problem, the result of damage to the text at this point, or has it wider implications for the child's future? Her ability to feed the baby has been regarded by some as evidence of Chrysis continuing to rear it even after the marriage of Moschion and Plangon; her inability to do so, because she never had a baby of her own, immediately rules out such a possibility and guarantees the child's return to its natural parents (see further 730 n.).

As in *Old Cantankerous* Menander proves remarkably sparing of names throughout the monologue, introducing his characters instead by their role and relationship to one another. Only Chrysis, the title role, stands as an exception to this, as Knemon did before.

60. I'll just wait...what they're talking about: A character withdrawing to one side in order to eavesdrop on those arriving on stage was a frequently used convention in New Comedy. In the present context, however, it becomes all the more pointed in so far as Moschion returns after so short an interval, 'the first of a long series of incidents in this play that cheat the expectations that have been aroused' as Sandbach[1] observes.

65. I've lost my nerve: On a technical level Moschion's collapse of nerve exists to introduce a plot based on Demeas' misinterpretation of what he finds when he returns home. In dramatic terms, on the other hand, it forms an element in establishing Moschion's overall character. In the opening monologue the young man had demonstrated a remarkable egotism; here we see an additional factor – passivity: his inability to initiate action, and his preference to allow things to happen, doubtless in the hope that problems will solve themselves, a trait shared with Aeschinus in Terence's *The Brothers* 688ff. In later scenes he manifests a similar inability to see the implications of his actions, unwittingly allowing blame for the problems he creates to settle onto the shoulders of others, in particular Chrysis, just as Pamphilus does in Terence's *The Mother-in-Law*. Only in Act V in fact does Moschion begin to initiate action, though by then his efforts are both unnecessary and totally misguided. At the same time his timorous reaction to the imminent return of his father ushers in the possibility of resistance to the idea of marriage on Demeas' part - somewhat illogical in view of the joint-venture with Nikeratos – but a common theme in New Comedy. Menander then turns such expectation of trouble to humour when the audience sees it negated by the marriage the two old men have already planned for their children (see futher Ireland[1]). Equally significant for potential development here is the role apparently given to Parmenon, whose reaction to Moschion's failure of nerve is reminiscent of the cunning slave so prominent in Roman Comedy, and exemplified in Menander by Daos in *The Shield*, ever-ready to step in and help his young master escape from his predicament. If Menander intended such an interpretation here, once again he amuses by the subsequent failure of Parmenon to live up to the part (cf. Getas in *Old Cantankerous*, Parmeno in Terence's *The Mother-in-Law*).

72f. wailing at this door here: The commonplace image of the helpless lover mooning around the front door of his beloved shut against him forms a natural element in Parmenon's exasperation, just as his desire to press on with the marriage and its traditional festive elements of garlands and sesame (an important ingredient of wedding cakes) indicates not so much his ignorance of the consent yet to be gained from Demeas and Nikeratos (cf. *Old Cantankerous* 760 n.) as his desire to counteract Moschion's reluctance to contribute any effort towards it.

77. What about the baby?: The papyrus nowhere identifies the speaker or provides clues as to punctuation. Editors are therefore divided over whether the words constitute a question, as in the translation, or an exhortation: 'Let's leave Chrysis here go on nursing it...', and whether they are spoken by Moschion or Parmenon. No less contentious is whether the passage provides any clue as to the originator of the plan to hand the baby over to Chrysis. Parmenon's later denial of any responsibility for the situation would seem to rule him out, leaving Moschion, who had formally acknowledged the child as his (54), or Chrysis who, unlike Moschion, displays remarkable loyalty to it in the rest of the action. On the other hand it may be that the playwright never intended to introduce consideration of the plan's origin, inviting his audience instead simply to accept the situation portrayed here.

80. He'll cool down again: False foreshadowing. Though the audience is induced to accept Chrysis' interpretation, within the complex web of misapprehension that develops and in which Groton sees a powerful undercurrent of violent emotion, it is Moschion's prediction of trouble that proves correct.

94. I'll go and practise: It is not accidental that Menander returns to the theme of Moschion's lost nerve and the difficulty of the situation immediately before the entry of Demeas and Nikeratos indicates development of quite a different scenario.

96. Demeas: As often in the play, the papyrus gives no indication of who speaks first when the two old men enter. Attribution of parts, therefore, is dependent upon analysis of what seems appropriate to each. That Demeas should initiate the dialogue, however, is suggested by both the greater prominence of his role in the play and the more forceful personality he consistently displays in comparison with Nikeratos. Similarly, the imaginative interpretation of the weather at Byzantium (110f.) seems well in accord with the equally imaginative interpretation of Plangon's pregnancy at 589ff. In contrast, reference to 'pure benefit of the poor' (101) is more appropriate to Nikeratos, who elsewhere displays characteristics of the poor man in his relations with Demeas: his resistance to Demeas' proposal in the fragmentary section 165-89 to hold the wedding that same day, the absence of any reference to porters accompanying him, the state of the sheep he provides for sacrifice at 399ff. and perhaps the absence of an immediate dowry at 727f. Similarly, the generally staccato style adopted in such statements as 'Black Sea...wormwood' is echoed elsewhere, including his reaction to finding Chrysis expelled from Demeas' house, 410ff. (see further Turner[1] p. 121f., Webster[2] p. 104).

Nowhere in the extant text does Menander provide any indication of why the two old men, apparently so different in their fortunes and in some aspects of their characters, should go abroad together, or why they have decided to link their families through the marriage of their children. As in the case of 77 it may well be that he never intended any explanation, presenting instead a situation for his audience to accept as a conventional starting point and to enjoy its further development. Certainly, suggestions that the proposed marriage was designed to remove Moschion as a rival to the affections of Chrysis, or that Nikeratos had somehow endeared himself to Demeas on their travels, are no more than spectres within commentators' imaginations. By the same token, though different from one another in many ways, the two characters do display a considerable degree of compatible interaction which allows them to provide foils for one another throughout, with Nikeratos, here as elsewhere, given the more overtly comic role.

100. wormwood: A herb noted for its bitterness. The assumption is that it was present in such abundance everything was tainted by it, cf. Plautus' *Trinummus* 934ff., Philostratos' *Life of Apollonius* I, 21, who observes that the huge quantities in Babylonia affected all the other edible wild plants there.

119. There are a few points...: Though the text breaks off at this point, the failure to set a date for the wedding there and then, together with the reference to a few points, may have been introduced to reinforce the image of Demeas as both tactful towards his neighbour and considerate of Moschion's feelings. The first of these has already manifested itself in his claim that the proposed marriage was his own idea (118), thereby avoiding any imputation of the poorer Nikeratos deliberately seeking an advantageous match for his daughter. The latter may have been further developed by a declaration of the need to consult with the young man first, and if this is the case, it would be wholly consistent with Demeas' tendency, so evident in the rest of the play, to have Moschion's welfare at heart.

Act II

The reappearance of Moschion closely followed by that of Demeas, allows Menander to bridge the interval between Acts both visually, by the reintroduction of a character just seen, and thematically, by the continuing contrast – humorous through its very incongruity – between Moschion's anxiety over raising the question of marriage and the preparations his father has already made for just such an event. Once again, the essential lack of initiative in Moschion's character comes to the fore. Though he left to prepare himself for the inevitable meeting with his father, he has allowed himself to lapse all too easily into reverie, totally neglecting the supposedly difficult task that stood between his desires and their fulfilment – all to his cost, as he now recognises. That lack of purpose, however, is essential to the plot if its complications are to be fully developed, while any unsympathetic reaction on the audience's part is mitigated by the conventional helplessness of the young man in love, cf. Chaireas in *The Shield*, Philolaches in Plautus' *The Ghost*, Antipho in Terence's *Phormio* or Ctesipho in *The Brothers*.

130. I seem to have acquired a wife: Demosthenes 59, 122 aptly sums up the basis of Demeas' annoyance: 'We have mistresses (*hetairai*) for pleasure, concubines (*pallakai*) for the day-to-day care of our bodies, and wives for the production of legitimate children and to look after things at home'. By ostensibly choosing to rear a child, therefore, Chrysis has clearly gone beyond what was expected of her as a *hetaira* (cf. Fantham p. 65f.). That Demeas should react with such sudden anger and then decide so precipitously to eject both mistress and child from his home (133f.) lays the foundation, in fact, for what will demonstrably be his major character weakness (cf. Goldberg[2] p. 96, Grant p. 182f.), one that he shares with Nikeratos in view of the resistance displayed at 176ff. (see 167ff. n.) and the events of Act IV. Where the two differ, however, lies in the additional depth and sophistication Menander injects into his depiction of Demeas, the fact that the old man's subsequent outbursts do not come out of the blue but after close, if ill-directed, interrogation and reasoning in the case of 321ff. and 359ff., and after a highly self-controlled attempt to protect his son's reputation at 481ff. In dramatic terms too, Demeas' anger here proves pivotal for development of the play. In retrospect it contradicts Chrysis' earlier assurances that love would conquer all. Instead it is Moschion who must suddenly face the problem he forecast at 80, defend a child the audience knows to be his own, and by extension prevent the expulsion of Chrysis. In terms of foreshadowing, on the other hand, the forced intervention of Moschion and his initial success suggest a shift to concentration upon the father–son axis in future action and a reduction of Chrysis' role to one that is essentially passive, a prey to Demeas' misapprehension and annoyance, and defended by nothing more substantial than the sophistry and misapplied favour of a young man whose personal embarrassment and inhibitions severely curtail his effectiveness. This, in turn, forms the foundation for development of the pathos in Chrysis' role, the fact that for all the consideration she has so far displayed it is she who is the real victim of circumstances, just as Sostrata is in Terence's *The Mother-in-Law*. Attempts by commentators to go beyond this, however, and to see in Demeas' outburst a determination to avoid any threat to Moschion's inheritance (impossible in so far as an illegitimate child – as any child of Chrysis' would inevitably be – was debarred from automatic inheritance in Attic law), or to suggest that Demeas had known of Chrysis' pregnancy before leaving and his annoyance was the result of finding his instructions to dispose of the baby disobeyed, are mere flights of fancy or imaginative restoration of gaps in the text. At best, Demeas' decision to expel Chrysis may represent a determination to regain mastery of his household in the face of events that conflict with social convention.

135. someone else: Though the reference is undoubtedly to Chrysis, the phrasing in the Greek – the irregular use of a *masculine* pronoun – adds an element of ambiguity. Goldberg[2] p. 96 suggests it is designed to emphasise Demeas' growing remoteness from his mistress, but at the same time the masculine gender also suggests an unwitting and ironic reference to Moschion, for whom the child is really being reared.

137. What's legitimacy or illegitimacy?: It is a telling mark of Moschion's indecision that at the very moment the threat to the child gives him a positive cue to reveal the truth, he prefers instead to engage in generalised sophistry based on arguments that were commonplace by Menander's time, cf. Euripides' *Andromache* 638 'many illegitimate folk are better than those born legitimate'.

151f. I hope you'll ask no questions...help me?: How are we to interpret Moschion's plea here and Demeas' reassuring response 'I understand, Moschion.'? If restoration of the damaged text is correct, it would be tempting to see in them a veiled hint to the liaison with Plangon, Demeas' recognition of it and his connivance with it; it would also totally contradict subsequent developments or, at best, represent the insertion of a blatant inconsistency for momentary effect. Instead, Moschion's eagerness for the marriage, which Demeas must have suggested unexpectedly in the missing lines, both continues the theme of the young man's character-weakness – his gratitude for an easy escape from the necessity of having to broach the subject himself – and introduces considerable potential for the development of irony. On one level, the declaration of sincerity seems specifically designed to cut short any surprise on Demeas' part at finding his son so anxious for a match ostensibly forced upon him. The inherent ambiguity of Moschion's phrasing on the other hand has quite a different significance for the audience. No less doubleedged is Demeas' reply, the momentary potential for embarrassment caused by his puzzled questions converted into relief at having seemingly achieved his son's compliance so easily. With even greater irony, however, Moschion's emphatic eagerness here becomes the cause of still worse trouble for Chrysis, when Demeas later interprets it as a device to escape the woman's clutches (333ff.).

161. He won't say no: The certainty is a result of Moschion's knowledge that he has Plangon and her mother on his side, an ironic contrast to Demeas' own prediction at 200, and one that mirrors the earlier instance between Moschion and Chrysis in Act I.

167ff.: From the fragmentary remains of the dialogue between Demeas and Nikeratos (omitted from the translation) it is clear that the task of gaining the old man's consent does not proceed with total ease. After raising the question of a date for the wedding, Demeas apparently broaches the possibility of holding the ceremony that very day (175). In response, a character, presumably Nikeratos, declares it to be impossible, though the precise details of why he should now object to something he has already agreed to are lost in the missing sections. A reference, however, to 'before informing friends' (181) may point to the suddenness of the suggestion as lying at the root of the problem, the difficulty of sending out invitations at such short notice. Following this, within the space of only a few lines, Demeas may have reminded his friend of some debt of gratitude owed (183), since in what follows, a character, again presumably Nikeratos, refers to giving way and perhaps the churlishness of raising objections (186f.), to which comes the response that he is now being sensible. Further possible objections – that Nikeratos' reluctance demonstrates his independence of Demeas along the lines of Gorgias at *Old Cantankerous* 821ff. – have been variously suggested, but too little remains to guarantee certainty.

198ff. I haven't a clue...orders: What is the point of introducing the theme of the slave's puzzlement here? Is it to emphasise at the end of the Act the degree to which Demeas has seized the initiative over others – over Moschion since 130 and now over Parmeno, who was earlier revealed as the prime force in urging forward the question of the wedding but is now reprimanded for his slowness? Is Menander in fact pioneering a reversal of conventional roles with the depiction of an ostensibly domineering slave reduced to a position of total subordination (cf. *The Arbitration* 557ff. n., Parmeno in Terence's *The Mother-in-Law*)?

Act III

Despite transient obstacles presented by Nikeratos, and Demeas' discovery of the child, the dramatic movement of the play so far has been consistently towards a marriage desired by all concerned. Nothing as yet constitutes that major element of complication to the play's goal so familiar from the rest of New Comedy. In reality, however, the ease with which the present situation has been reached belies its inherent instability; for it is founded upon a state of misapprehension, if not outright deceit, and has at its heart a rupture of natural justice involving both the status of the child and Demeas' perception of Chrysis' present role. By the same token, immediate revelation of the truth would inevitably bring the action to a premature conclusion. As a result, Acts III and IV exist to force present circumstances to a state of crisis before a proper resolution can be effected. Once again, however, for all the disparity between the dramatic spirit of Acts II and III, Menander continues to employ his bridging technique, not only in the person of Demeas, but also on a thematic level in the further development of preparations for the marriage ceremony.

207. a storm: Before detailing the events that have caused the sudden change in Demeas' mood, Menander is careful to establish the atmosphere of shock felt at recent events through the introduction of the commonplace image of the storm, cf. Euripides' *Heracleidae* 427ff., Plautus' *The Ghost* 737ff.

214. I'm coming down-stage to you: If restoration of the damaged text is correct, this rupture in the dramatic illusion underlines on one level the essential artificiality of stage monologues (as opposed to true soliloquies), their main function being to provide the audience with information in a concentrated form. In this respect, indeed, Demeas' monologue has affinities with the messenger speech of tragedy, designed to bring offstage events before the audience. Nevertheless, Menander displays no small skill in turning the very artificiality of the device to advantage; for instead of the old man stepping out of character by his reference to the audience, he actually draws it into the quasi-reality of the play by placing it in the role of confidant as he struggles to control his emotions. No less indicative of the playwright's skill is the strategic placing of the audience address, which marks the transition from initial preparations 'with everything going according to plan' to the preliminaries of disaster, characterised as these are by the dichotomy between expectation and result, cf. Terence's *The Mother-in-Law* 365ff. Similarly the briefer reference 'Ladies and Gentlemen' at 269 (lit. 'Gentlemen' cf. *Old Cantankerous* 194 n.) marks a similar shift from narrative to reflection and rising emotion (though with the additional irony that the appeal is addressed to an audience that knows the truth), thus establishing an overall tripartite structure within the speech (see further Blundell p. 36).

219ff. The minute I went in...: Demeas' account of events inside is carefully structured to tantalise. Though Menander has generated an atmosphere of impending trouble in the monologue's preliminaries, he delays reference to what has actually caused the old man's shock for another thirty lines with details that are at once comic because of their very banality and yet, as in many a modern 'thriller', create tension by their retarding effect. How for instance is the 'knock-out blow' of 215 to emerge from a description of culinary preparations, the checking of supplies, and the arrival on the scene of an old nurse? Is the very concentration upon superfluous and extraneous details, such as the supplies required or the function of the room next to the pantry, an indication of Demeas' shock – his loss of proper perspective and the ability to tell what is relevant to the narrative?

237f. She was once my slave: The description of the nurse, with her freedom as the reward for long service, serves to reinforce the picture of Demeas established at the outset as an essentially generous and kind-hearted figure, one whose later harsh treatment of Chrysis is as much an aberration as that of Tyndarus by Hegio in Plautus' *The Prisoners*. At the same time, the whole account is strongly suffused with elements of comic coincidence, irony and contrast. The first two we see in Menander's use of the very figure who once nursed Moschion to create disaster for the nurse of the young man's own offspring. Contrast on the other hand can be seen in (1) the dichotomy between the intentions behind the old woman's burblings over the baby and their effect, and (2) the juxtaposition of opposites in terms of mood and movement. As Sandbach[1] observes in the case of mood, 'her commonplaces...provide a background of banality against which her bombshell explodes'. The second is termed by Goldberg[2] p. 98 'the blending of static and dynamic portraits': the old woman's careless chatter contrasted with the other servant's hasty entry and anxious whispers (255ff.), a contrast given further colour by the direct quotation of their words. Such an entry by the servant-girl serves in fact a double function: (1) It cuts short the nurse's chatter at the point where Demeas possesses only half the truth. (2) By her reaction to the old woman's revelations (cf. Demeas' 'She didn't know I was inside, but thought she could speak safely' in 240f.) it ensures an aura of conspiratorial secrecy that helps convince him of the information's accuracy and in turn affects his approach to his second source of information, Parmenon, at 295ff.

265. my Samian: Reference to Chrysis by her point of origin rather than by name once again signals a distancing of Demeas from her, similar to that at the beginning of Act II.

271. I'm not angry – not yet: The disclaimer suggests an even more serious situation than 129ff., since it introduces an element of deliberate calculation into any response in contrast to the pure emotion evident earlier. Behind Demeas' precarious self-control is the conflicting evidence that assails his senses. On the one hand he *hears* of Moschion's paternity from a source he can only presume is objective, information, however, that runs counter to everything he knows about his son. On the other hand, the *sight* of Chrysis nursing the child confirms the assumption he has had ever since his return home: that the infant belongs to his mistress. Menander is careful, however, not to squander the potential effect of Demeas' discovery by dramatic development that is too precipitate. For the moment, its function is the production of shock and dismay; only later, following apparent confirmation of his worst fears, does it become the cue for the anger here repressed to convert itself into action.

279. fit to be tied: lit. 'out of my mind'.

283. Parmenon: The return of the slave and his interaction with a stock comic character such as the cook are not fortuitous. Demeas' earlier monologue had raised the spectre of trust betrayed, a theme of such potential seriousness that the old man had been unable to give voice to it or even to formulate it fully as a thought. In many respects it is more reminiscent of tragic plots like Euripides' *Hippolytos* than of New Comedy, and as a result has to be diverted for the moment by the insertion of conventional humour in the form of the cook's fussy loquaciousness (cf. *Old Cantankerous* 393 n., 412), which forms an island of respite in a process of ever deepening gloom.

285. slicing through everything with your tongue: cf. *Old Cantankerous* 399 n.

293. In case you haven't noticed: lit. 'If you haven't noticed'. Parmenon's exasperation echoes in fact the long series of 'if's' in the cook's previous statement: five in the Greek.

297. Sure: Like his later self-important instructions to Chrysis when he reappears at 301ff. and his optimistic 'At your service, sir!', Parmenon's assurance here is designed to contrast with the storm the audience knows is brewing, and to justify Demeas' belief in 298f. that the slave is bound to know the full story.

302f. keep the old crone...wine-bottles!: A conventional jibe at the alcoholic tendencies of old women in New Comedy and directed in all probability against Moschion's former nurse, cf. *Old Cantankerous* 855ff.

304. away from the door: Why does Demeas wish to move the interrogation of Parmenon away from his own front door? Is it so as not to be overheard and thus give advance warning to those inside, as on other occasions when the topic for discussion is confidential?

306f. I don't *want* to beat you: To ensure continuation and constant deepening of Demeas' misapprehension, the playwright arranges for the old man to be given no opportunity to learn the truth either in the present interrogation, or later from Chrysis, even though it is clearly in the interests of both to reveal it when faced by the old man's anger. This is especially the case with Parmenon, who has no ulterior motive, such as attachment to the child, that might induce him to sacrifice his own interests. Demeas' initial reference to a beating therefore is specifically designed (1) to put the slave on his guard and thus to reveal as little as possible, presumably in case any information volunteered might produce the very result Demeas here threatens, and (2) to confirm in Demeas' mind from Parmenon's reaction that he is indeed the victim of his household's conspiracy. So it is that after the old man's declaration 'I know' (311) Parmenon is grudgingly forced to concede information: from the position agreed at 77ff. to the revelation of Moschion's role (316-20). The result, however, is not clarity but a convergence of ironic misunderstanding – Demeas', that Parmenon, who 'knows everything', has confirmed his worst fears, Parmenon's that his master's claim to complete understanding is borne out by the partial disclosure in 317f. From the audience's standpoint the dialogue becomes doubly effective precisely because of the ambiguity inherent in the claims made by both sides: Demeas' claim, for instance, that 'Chrysis is nursing it (the child) now for his (Moschion's) sake', which betokens parenthood to the one, no more than feeding to the other; Parmenon's 'we didn't want it to get out', which from the slave's viewpoint refers only to news of Plangon's rape and Nikeratos' reaction should he learn of it, but which to Demeas confirms the Moschion–Chrysis conspiracy to cuckold him. With partial revelation on both sides, therefore, the stage is soon reached where anger earlier repressed can be given full rein, preventing any further opportunity for, or possibility of, clarification as Parmenon is driven from the stage.

309f. by angels...of heaven – : lit. Dionysos, god of wine, Apollo, Zeus Saviour, and Asclepios, god of healing.

324. I've a rod in pickle for you: lit. 'you scoundrel worthy of a whipping'.

325ff. O citadel...upper lip: As Goldberg[2] p. 100f. observes, while Demeas' earlier monologue was essentially serious, the present one, for all its tragic overtones, is lightened by the very style in which it is couched. The appeal with which it opens, for instance, (a quotation from Euripides' lost play *Oedipus* according to a marginal note in the papyrus) provides a histrionic outburst humorous because of its very inappropriateness, and made all the more so by the bathos of Demeas' self-correction (cf. Sostratos in *Old Cantankerous* 214f., Blundell p. 65ff.). Similarly, its movement from outrage to controlled determination balances the previous speech where the flow was from controlled narrative to the momentary outburst of 279 'I'm absolutely fit to be tied'.

328. It's not *Moschion*...wrong: An incongruous claim in view of the evidence at Demeas' disposal, and made all the more comic by involving in his tortuous reasoning an audience fully aware of how mistaken he is. As Goldberg[2] p. 101 observes, Demeas appeals to logic, yet his logic is flawed by misapprehension stemming directly from emotion – the rage that drove Parmenon from the stage. He champions a son whose previous good behaviour (ironic in itself) induces him to regard Moschion's enthusiasm for marriage as an attempt to escape the clutches of Chrysis – instead of what the audience knows is the grateful relief of a weak-willed adolescent desperate to avoid the embarrassment of his own actions. Similarly, Demeas reviles his mistress not because of any objective blame attached to her but simply because her 'guilt' follows directly from the presumption of Moschion's innocence. This concern for the young man Menander is careful to underpin, however, with the theme of Moschion's adoptive status (346). Just as the act of adoption was the result of a deliberate decision and Demeas' previous indulgence was designed to reinforce the bond between father and son, so the decision to take Moschion's side is based on a determination to maintain that bond even at the price of losing Chrysis, just as earlier he had apparently risked losing her to younger rivals rather than risk embarrassment. The potential for tragic pathos in such a situation cannot be ignored, but it is a potential the playwright diverts into comedy by the preposterous error upon which Demeas' reasoning is based and his patent reversal of normal comic convention; for while the combination of young blood and wine is the preliminary to illicit sexual activity in a number of plays (cf. Plautus' *The Pot of Gold*), Demeas here makes Moschion the victim rather than the more normal perpetrator.

337. that Helen of mine: Helen of Troy, whose elopement with Paris made her an archetypal unfaithful wife. Here, as in 348 'she's a trollop. She's poison' and 354 'the fair Samian', Demeas' refusal to call Chrysis by name continues the process of distancing himself from her (cf. 265) as a preliminary to driving her from the house. At the same time, however, Menander is careful to mitigate the potential seriousness of Demeas' intentions by indicating the genuineness of the old man's affection for Chrysis (350ff.). If anything, the vehemence of his denunciation is itself evidence of his love, which he thinks has now been betrayed, and of the wrench which his rejection of her constitutes. From this in turn stems the presumption that his love will be amply restored once the misapprehension he labours under is removed. In this respect Demeas mirrors the behaviour of Polemon in *The Rape of the Locks* and this finds further echoes in the rejection of their wives by Charisios in *The Arbitration* and Pamphilus in Terence's *The Mother-in-Law*.

355f. No need to give any other reason: Demeas' decision to resurrect the anger of 130ff. becomes both the means by which Menander is able to prevent the old man's true motivation emerging and the harbinger of further irony when Moschion attempts to repeat his earlier defence (cf. the use Pamphilus makes of the supposed enmity between his mother and wife in Terence's *The Mother-in-Law*).

357. Cook: The emergence of the cook at this point is accounted for in the first instance by purely technical considerations: to avoid an empty stage while Demeas is indoors, and to ensure he is in place when his role does eventually become dramatic – during the expulsion. There his purpose is clearly to lighten the scene and to set the comic tone for an essentially tragic event, a function already foreshadowed in the description of Demeas as 'A maniac with a grey beard' (361) and 'loopy' (363), and in the preoccupation with the safety of his crockery (365f.).

372f. You've got...crone: Presumably Moschion's old nurse who, like the maids promised at 381f., is reduced virtually to the status of a trinket. The intention of the reference is perhaps to demonstrate Demeas' generosity in allowing his ex-mistress to leave with more than she deserves, and certainly more than she came with, cf. Plautus' *The Swaggering Soldier* 981f.

374. Is it because I kept the baby?: As earlier, Menander skilfully formulates the exchange so that Chrysis is given neither the opportunity nor the motivation to advance beyond Demeas' misapprehension; hence her question here is made to echo in its phrasing the old man's words at 354f. Within the overall purpose of the dialogue, however, the playwright momentarily toys with his audience's expectations (cf. *Old Cantankerous* 784ff.), raising the fleeting prospect of further devastating revelation as a result of Demeas' response at 374 'Yes and because...', before the old man checks himself, refuses any further details and then directs the dialogue away from the baby altogether and onto the safer ground of his mistress' supposed ingratitude. For Chrysis herself, Demeas' evasiveness reduces her role in the exchange to little more than that of cue for development of the old man's complaints of trust betrayed, exemplified as these are by a tone of curt sarcasm in which her very name, so studiously avoided in the earlier monologue, becomes in 378, 382, and 392, a barb to use against her. Further structuring of the dialogue is injected by the asides and attempted interventions of the cook, which mark, or perhaps even disguise, the shifts that take place in Demeas' thought processes: from the baby to Chrysis' ingratitude marked by the aside at 375, and from this to predictions of her future life marked by the attempted intervention of 382-90.

390. Once you're on the town: The final picture of Chrysis' life in the future as a *hetaira* who has failed to gain the more permanent security of concubine marks the low-point of the whole scene, unalleviated by the cook and only rescued from total blackness by the arrival of Nikeratos, whose preoccupation with the sheep links him to the conventional comedy associated with such animals (cf. *Old Cantankerous* 393ff.). Why, though, if Nikeratos' role is to lighten the atmosphere here and to provide Chrysis with a place of refuge, thus clearing the stage at the end of the Act, did Menander not introduce him earlier, in place of the cook? Is he, as Goldberg[2] p. 22 suggests, too absurd a figure to have been included earlier without necessitating a more prominent part and thus affecting the scene's undoubtedly serious tone, or did Menander wish to hold him in reserve until the explosive events of Act IV?

399. will satisfy the ritual demands: The description of the sheep contains the implication that it has little else to offer, that while the gods will receive those (otherwise inedible) parts usually reserved for them, there will be little left for any human banquet (cf. *Old Cantankerous* 451ff., Plautus' *The Pot of Gold* 561ff.). The purpose of the description, however, is not to portray Nikeratos as too miserly to buy anything better, as was once thought, but rather to stress the frugality of his means – this is all he can afford.

411f. Sheer lunacy!...easy-going chap: The close proximity of the two statements produces an interesting contrast in Nikeratos' characterisation and thinking. He possesses what Sandbach[1] describes as 'the realism of the poor', criticising Chrysis for undertaking to rear a child when she had no independent means of supporting it and no guarantee that her protector would accept it. No less than Chrysis at 80, however, Nikeratos is led by his knowledge of Demeas to see an easy resolution of current difficulties (420), equally wrongly though; for as the audience knows, he too is totally unaware of the revolution that has taken place in

Demeas' view of the situation. In many respects, the closing lines of Act III also contain a considerable degree of irony and foreshadowing: irony in the picture of one grandfather rescuing a child his other grandfather has just rejected, foreshadowing in the reversal of anger and calm that takes place towards the end of Act IV and is echoed in the very language used: 'He's out of his mind' (416), 'He's raving mad' (563).

Act IV

As the vehicle for development of the play's ultimate crisis and its resolution, Act IV sees not only a rise in the overall tempo of presentation, with the change from normal dialogue metre (iambic trimeter) to the livelier trochaic tetrameter, but also the introduction of a series of dramatic contrasts. The first of these opens the Act itself – a radical shift from Nikeratos' assurances at the end of Act III to his agitation at the upset now created in his own household, upset made all the more ironic since it stems directly from his decision to give Chrysis refuge. It is followed by the comic contrast of Moschion's continuing preoccupation with himself and the marriage – his attempts to kill time with constant bathing and the joke on the tardy arrival of evening (cf. Plautus' *Amphitryo* 271ff.), together with his eagerness to fetch his bride, not even bothering in his impatience to return Nikeratos' greeting at 431. This in turn separates Nikeratos' upset from the complaints soon to come from Demeas, and for much the same reason – the expulsion and its repercussions for a marriage both old men are still striving to complete.

437. Because of the baby: This forms the third stage (after the episodes with Parmenon and Chrysis) by which Menander ensures continuation of the misapprehension that underlies Demeas' assessment of the situation and upon which the play's complication is founded. By this point, each of the characters party to the conspiracy developed in Act I has either been neutralised as a potential source of objective information, by being driven from the stage, or is deflected into a totally erroneous interpretation of the old man's anger.

440f. I'll knock tears out of you all right: As Sandbach[1] observes, Demeas' threat is somewhat paradoxical since it is designed actually to end the tears of his household.

444. Lord: Apollo Agyieus (protector of the street) as at 309, his presence outside houses being represented by a pillar or altar.

451. you tackle him first: The result not of any sudden collapse of nerve on Nikeratos' part compared to the annoyance of 427, but of the need to shift attention to the father–son axis, which forms the true centre of dramatic action. Despite the smallness of Nikeratos' speaking role until 492, however, his very presence continues to exert a powerful influence upon the contents of the dialogue, deflecting Demeas away from any proper explanation of his anger at the very point this might have become a possibility (463), and forcing him to continue the attempt to preserve Moschion's reputation – despite the young man's own apparent indifference. Later it exerts the same effect upon Moschion, when at 489 his father positively invites clarification. Menander further emphasises the inability of father and son to communicate openly, and the deep dichotomy that exists in their perception of the situation by the series of asides which brings their reactions to one another's arguments before the audience.

453. Chrysis: Is it mere chance that Moschion is made to employ Chrysis' name here, at 472 and at 479 (the instance at 464 in the translation does not exist in the Greek), when Demeas had been so careful to avoid it earlier or had used it virtually as a term of abuse? Or is its positioning a pointer to a tripartite division in the dialogue, each step marking a rise in the emotional temperature: (1) enquiries into the cause of the expulsion, (2) Moschion's insistence that Chrysis join the wedding celebrations, and (3) the young man's defence of her in the context of what Demeas sees as a liaison between them?

458f. What do you imagine your friends will say: In the light of Demeas' interpretation of recent events and his attempt to preserve his son's reputation the question is highly ironic. Later we find it mirrored in more comical form by Nikeratos' own self-congratulatory imaginings at 510ff.

460. I'd be failing in my duty: The words hark back to 134ff. where Moschion's sententious defence of the child operated on the same high moral plane he attempts to establish here, though clearly with less success.

464. Nikeratos...to come back here: Moschion's attempt to abandon persuasion and to seize the initiative through action is based upon a twofold misapprehension:

1) his belief that Demeas' recent actions are founded upon nothing more than a resurgence of his earlier annoyance, which can be overcome as easily now as it was at the beginning of Act II;

2) the presumption that his father's indulgent attitude, outlined in the play's opening monologue, can be made to reassert itself if enough pressure is brought to bear on him.

It is this latter factor that probably lies behind such statements as 'Yes I will' (461), 'Then grant it to me as a favour' (468) and 'I insist upon it' (473).

478. I was told by Parmenon: Demeas' reference to the slave as the source of his information creates considerable dramatic irony for an audience aware of how restricted and misunderstood the revelations of 306ff. actually were. Once again the exchange is constructed so as to give the semblance of total knowledge without the reality, resulting inevitably in an explosion of double meanings.

489. Tell Nikeratos: With his anger fuelled by the brazenness of his son's apparent admission, Demeas now does what he has so far studiously attempted to avoid – involve a third party in the situation, cf. Terence's *The Mother-in-Law* 698. To Moschion, of course, the choice of Plangon's father as witness is particularly inopportune – the first occasion in which the identity of the child's mother has specifically been raised in this form.

494. That's me done for now: Moschion interprets the vehemence of Nikeratos' outburst as evidence that the old man realises the truth about Plangon. Only subsequently, as a result of the analogies Nikeratos introduces, together with the reference to defilement of his bed (507) and to selling the other guilty party (508f.), does he begin to realise his mistake. For the moment, however, as Sandbach[1] observes, Moschion is actually saved from having to admit the truth by Nikeratos' intervention.

495f. Tereus, Oedipus, Thyestes: These were all perpetrators of forbidden love-intrigues: Tereus who seduced his wife's sister, Oedipus who in ignorance married his mother, and Thyestes who seduced the wife of his brother Atreus. As at 325ff., however, the tone of high tragedy inherent in the analogies is soon transformed into comedy by the bathos of Nikeratos' reference to a local Lothario (Menander refers in fact to an otherwise unknown Diomnestos who may have had such a reputation at the time) and to barbers' shops, traditional places for the exchange of gossip. No less comic is the reaction of Moschion himself as he is confronted with increasingly serious charges and must face the loss of the girl he loves, as much through his silence now as would earlier have been the case had he confessed the truth at 490f.

498. Amyntor's rage: There may be an element of irony in Nikeratos' reference. Most Athenians would gain their knowledge of myths from the tragedies they saw on the stage, in particular those of Euripides, who by Menander's time had become the most popular of tragedians. In his play *Phoinix*, however, it was Amyntor's concubine, Phthia, who attempted to seduce the young man and, when she failed, falsely accused him of the act, whereupon Amyntor blinded him.

526. I'll be cleared of the more serious charge: The essential weakness of Moschion's character is graphically illustrated by the fact that even now he only reveals the truth in order to avoid a still worse charge, his continuing embarrassment underlined by Demeas' annoyed rejoinder 'You'll be the death of me...'. This same embarrassment, however, first seen in the monologue that opened the play, soon serves the additional, if somewhat mundane, function of removing Moschion from the stage at 539, thereby allowing concentration upon the more dramatically effective old men.

532. O misery, misery me!: Nikeratos' frantic reappearance introduces a further instance of disappointed audience expectations after the outburst at 519 and an episode intended to parody many of the developments seen in Act III. Instead of the careful and deliberate self-control of 262ff., designed to prevent anyone from realising Demeas' discovery and its implications for him, we see wild distraction from Nikeratos and a veritable obsession with revealing the disgrace that has come upon his family. Just as in the earlier episode it was Demeas who had been caused distress, while Nikeratos with his sheep was comically calm and ready to provide a refuge for Chrysis, now it is Nikeratos who is enraged, even if the manifestation of that rage tends to the ridiculous, and Demeas who must attempt to provide the calming influence. Just as Demeas had hurled against Parmenon at 317 a charge of conspiracy, so Nikeratos' second appearance brings with it similar accusations. Once again, though, Nikeratos' exaggerated threats, the ineffectiveness of his actions indoors and the almost Plautine rapidity of his movements ensure a totally comic ambiance. Even the motivation behind his entry at 563 'I just wanted to warn you' has its element of irony in the belief that Demeas' attitude remains unchanged from 518; so unaware is Nikeratos of the extent to which it has in fact changed.

537. I've wronged you: With the role of the angry and foolish old man now firmly assumed by Nikeratos, Demeas is able to revert to being the sorrowing father, a change important for future developments in the contrast it provides with Moschion's inability to reciprocate his father's openness and regret and his peevish determination to exact revenge.

540f. Breast-feeding...daughter: After the momentary distraction of Demeas' apology and Moschion's retreat from the stage the verbatim repetition of 535f. (though in reverse word-order) both emphasises the degree of Nikeratos' shock and refocuses attention back onto the old men.

547. He's gone: Following Nikeratos' departure indoors again Demeas takes on the role filled at 360ff. by the cook (cf. Sikon in *Old Cantankerous* 639ff.), commenting on the situation and the noises emanating from inside with the hyperbolic condemnation of his own role (551f.) and the melodramatic prospect of a roast grandson.

559. she's grabbed the baby: The introduction of Chrysis at this point serves a number of purposes:

1) It restores the link between the child and the figure who throughout the action has posed as its protector, a link temporarily interrupted by

54

Plangon's nursing.

2) It ensures that the baby's return to Demeas' house does not necessitate the appearance on stage of Plangon, which would have ruptured the conventional avoidance of bringing such girls before the audience in New Comedy.

3) It restores the situation to the expulsion demanded by Demeas at 518, upon which further dramatic developments can be based.

4) It provides a comic mirror scene for the earlier expulsion, with Chrysis once again the victim of one old man rescued by another.

568. Help!: Since the threat to Chrysis and the child has been developed at some length and in terms of considerable, albeit comic, violence (it is probably Chrysis whom Nikeratos threatens to kill at 560 not his own wife, though the Greek is ambiguous at this point – no doubt deliberately so), her return to safety is given similar scope by the insertion of eleven speaking parts between her appearance here and her re-entry into Demeas' house. Menander may also have intended a degree of hesitation on Chrysis' part to accept the old man's offer in view of her earlier experience.

578. Blackmailer!: The exclamation implies that Demeas is making gratuitous and false charges against Nikeratos and threatening court action to make him desist from his attempts to seize the baby.

579. It's *mine*: Commentators have made more of this claim than it deserves. Rather than signalling continued protection of Moschion's reputation by reversion to the now defunct fiction of Demeas' paternity or representing him as the child's protector, the assertion points simply to the irony of a situation in which both old men claim what will ultimately belong to neither. True, Demeas' assertion does have validity in law since he remains Moschion's and, through him, the baby's legal guardian, but to see this at work in the context of a heated argument is to inject unwanted precision. Demeas' claim, therefore, exists not to establish anything positive, but merely to negate Nikeratos' demand which precedes it.

585. Your son's hocussed me: At what stage does Nikeratos realise the connection between Moschion, Plangon and the child? Logic suggests this should have occured the moment he saw his daughter feeding the baby, since the outburst at 492ff. had already established Moschion's paternity in his mind. Such a scenario, however, would not only have demanded a more rapid resolution of the situation upon which the second half of Act IV is founded, but would have effectively removed any potential for comic development such as we have just witnessed. Rather than logic, therefore, Menander chooses to stress the shock of Nikeratos' discovery and the frantic emotions it produces. Only when this has been fully exploited does the playwright allow further progress in the drama with the question of the child's father. But is it here that the connection between Moschion and Plangon is made, or at 599 where the sentiment is repeated, or at 612, the closest the old man comes in the Act to an open accusation of rape? Commentators are divided. To Keuls[2] p. 12f. the accusation both here and at 599 indicates little more than Nikeratos' belief that Moschion is the prime author of the plot to conceal the birth of Plangon's child. More likely, however, realisation comes at 585 but its essentially serious implications are immediately deflected both by Demeas' assurances for the future and by the very ambiguity that surrounds its introduction (cf. Jacques p. 41 n.1, Bain[3] *ad loc.*). Hence, at what is the dénouement of the play Menander relies upon his audience's superior knowledge to obviate any need for explicit reference to the rape, concentrating instead upon winning Nikeratos over to acceptance of what he cannot change and restoration of his mental equilibrium, hardly an inconsiderable task, as the repeated assurance of 599 shows. In this, Demeas' fanciful reference to showers of gold and contemporary analogies serve not to indicate Nikeratos' stupidity, but to lighten the atmosphere and allow a return to the comic presentation of the old man, who had earlier accepted without demur Demeas' equally fanciful explanation of Byzantine weather. Only at 612, once Nikeratos has grudgingly accepted the situation, does the playwright allow a more explicit reference to Moschion's behaviour, when it can do no real harm.

590f. Zeus...seduced a girl who'd been locked up?: Danaë, only daughter of Acrisios, who locked her in a tower to escape his prophesied death at the hands of a grandson. The attempt to maintain her virginity was nullified, however, by Zeus entering through the roof as a shower of gold. The resultant infant, Perseus, was then set adrift with his mother in a chest, but was rescued and, when he grew to manhood, he did indeed kill his grandfather accidentally with a discus.

595f. How quickly we've found the solution!: The statement ingeniously invites Nikeratos' acquiescence by making him co-author of the solution Demeas offers.

606. Androcles: This otherwise unknown figure allows insertion of a double joke based on the picture of (1) an old man who desperately maintains the appearance and liveliness of youth, and (2) someone whose age and irritatingly constant presence makes him seem almost immortal.

610. My son...his bride: False foreshadowing, for though this was Moschion's hope in 159 and 433, he is himself soon to become the final obstacle to the happy ending.

612. But if I'd caught him then – : Nikeratos' parting shot, with its threat of serious consequences for Moschion under other circumstances (Harrison p. 36), is introduced not to suggest any diminution in his assent to the marriage, but to indicate he remains neither fully convinced by

Demeas' diversionary tactics nor totally reconciled to the position of victim Moschion's actions have imposed upon him, thus preparing for his role in Act V.

Act V

Though the close of Act IV saw an end to the obstacles that have so far stood in the way of the play's ultimate goal – the wedding – the fact that it did not also see an end to the play itself indicates that as in the case of *Old Cantankerous* there remain elements of the plot still requiring resolution. These manifest themselves in the need to include Moschion once more in the reinstated marriage ceremony after his hurried departure at 539, to restore relationships to the state they were in at the beginning of the play, and to develop the theme of natural justice by bringing Moschion, like Aeschinus in Terence's *The Brothers*, face to face with the deficiencies in his behaviour and his attitudes. By the same token, the fact that such developments take place in the final Act has its own implications for the atmosphere in which they are set and the form they take, in particular the emphasis upon the development of comedy and irony as the prime dramatic effects.

619f. But now...I'm furious: Anger after reflection is in many ways a characteristic Moschion shares with Demeas, but whereas Demeas has by now learned the error of his ways, his son lapses into feelings of injured pride. Similarly, though Moschion claims to be angry, the form in which he expresses himself belies the validity of the emotion: instead of the short staccato statements we might have expected and which Menander introduces with telling irony in the speech from Parmenon which follows, we find long meandering sentences. Instead of jumbled syntactic structure denoting agitation, there is oratorical precision and order. Instead of disconnection in the presentation of thoughts, there is careful balance: 'Just now.... But now...' (616-9), 'If it weren't for the problem.... But no such heroics now...' (623-30).

622. my father could have thought...behaviour: Moschion's sense of grievance, already prepared for by Demeas' confession at 537f., stems ironically from the high regard in which he holds his relationship with his father. The manner in which it is given expression, however, continues to reveal the young man's obsession with himself: his insistence upon regarding everything from the viewpoint of his own interests, oblivious to his role in producing the present situation, which stems directly from his blatant failure to fulfil the promise made at 76. As Goldberg[2] p. 104f.

aptly states, 'He refuses to admit to himself that Demeas' momentary injustice to him was a natural consequence of his own irresponsible desire to hide the truth'.

623. If it weren't…girl: Further evidence that Moschion's anger is in reality little more than pique. Rather than a declaration of action, his first decision is in fact to rule out any action by a declaration of its impossibility – his love for Plangon prevents him from being a free agent (631f.), forcing him instead to limit his planned revenge to the sham of pretence. Indeed, Menander produces in this an effective contrast between father and son; for whereas Demeas had been prepared to sacrifice his genuine feelings of love for Chrysis in order to protect his son, Moschion rejects any sacrifice as the price of success in punishing his father. Such a failure of resolve forms in many ways a precursor of the subsequent failure he encounters when attempting to put his plan into effect.

628f. the Foreign Legion: lit. Bactria and Caria. Sandbach[1] points out the irony of the contrast: Bactria on the very edge of the Greek World, Caria the closest region to Athens in which employment as a mercenary might be sought.

641ff. Parmenon: The slave's role in this final Act serves (1) to reinforce the unreality of Moschion's position through contrast; for while both share a sense of grievance at the treatment they have received from others, the reality of the slave's complaints and the matter-of-fact style he adopts in expressing them undercut the validity of Moschion's earlier outpourings; (2) to underline in Parmenon's puzzled reaction to Moschion's instructions (657-63) the incongruity of military plans in the context of the young man; and (3) by providing news of developments indoors to present Moschion with the possibility that his pretended departure will either fail by not attracting the attention of others, or be forced into reality because their reactions turn out to be quite the opposite of those initially envisaged.

651. One of our household: By this oblique reference to Chrysis, like the avoidance of any other name but his own in the Greek text at this point, Parmenon attempts to introduce an element of objectivity into the points he makes.

658. Stop this nonsense: The brusqueness of the instruction indicates both Moschion's impatience as he returns to dramatic focus after Parmenon's monologue and his continuing self-absorption as he casts aside the slave's complaints as irrelevant. Similarly, his command that Parmenon go inside even before being told what he is to do there provides a further pointer to the unreality of what is being planned.

661. and keep quiet about it: This is a strange instruction considering that Moschion's revenge positively requires Parmenon to attract attention as he fetches the cloak and sword. Commentators have variously sought to explain the discrepancy, suggesting that in stressing the need for secrecy, Moschion hopes Parmenon will do the exact opposite, or that the Greek refers to the immediate context, i.e., 'go and do what I tell you *and no more questions*', or that it is designed to prevent Demeas discovering the slave's mission until he has actually secured the items Moschion wants. More likely its insertion foreshadows the failure of the planned action through the very incongruity of the order.

664. Father'll come out now: In the context of a situation so divorced from reality such an overtly optimistic forecast positively invites disaster. Menander is careful to ensure the comic potential of failure is fully exploited, however, by depicting it in stages: first, Parmenon's discoveries inside, which lead him to disobey Moschion's instructions and to reappear without the cloak and sword; second, the slave's return at 687, having done all that was asked of him – brought the equipment *and* kept quiet about it – but with the net result the same and the plan no further forward.

670. You're quite out of date: The change of metre from that of spoken dialogue (iambic trimeters) to longer lines (trochaic tetrameters) indicates both an increase in tempo as the play moves into its final stages and an atmosphere of greater comedy as Parmenon now finds that his better understanding allows him to assert himself once again.

676. Why not fetch the bride right away?: In contrast to his earlier impatience to do just that, Moschion's absorption with his planned revenge makes him blind and deaf to the truth now presented by Parmenon and to his own best interests; hence the repeated insistence upon the sword and cloak (673, 675), his anger in 677ff. when the slave persists in his attempts to break through the young man's imaginings, his repeated rejection of the truth in 682 'Tell me something new' (echoing as it does his similar rejection of the slave's words at 658) and the slapstick that presents visually the young man's foolishness.

682. *Now* he'll come out: A deliberate echo of 664 signalling the next stage in Moschion's discomfiture, his recognition that the scenario envisaged earlier might actually be reversed and he be forced to make a choice between self-imposed exile and an embarrassing climb-down. In typical New Comedy fashion, however, neither possibility materialises. Instead, at the very moment Moschion's plan to lure his father outside and humiliate him lies in ruins, the old man appears of his own accord, wrests the intiative from his son, and by steering events in an altogether different direction begins the process of rescuing him from the impasse he has created for himself. Following this, the arrival on stage of Nikeratos further deflects the young man's embarrassment away from any overt regret for his earlier folly by introducing an element of external compulsion.

695f. I'm not surprised that you're hurt: An instance of dramatic economy in that Menander endows Demeas with the same understanding of Moschion's thought processes as the audience possesses. In this way the tension and momentum of these closing sections is maintained without the need for discursive explanations. The young man's foolishness is now further underlined by the very moderation and calmness of Demeas' reactions, which effectively cut the ground from under Moschion's feet by what amounts to a voluntary repetition of the apology at 537 without the need for any threatened departure to foreign parts. At the same time, by seizing the initiative, Demeas also highlights Moschion's own wrong-headedness in the relative scale of their reactions to events: faced by ostensible betrayal Demeas nevertheless attempted to protect his son's reputation; Moschion in contrast has sought to embarrass his father because of a single day's problems after a lifetime of kindness and in consequence has threatened his own personal happiness.

713. Everything's *been* done: The final task of the action is to restore momentum towards completion of the wedding; hence its prominence in the disgruntled statements of Nikeratos. At the same time the old man's appearance on stage forms a mirror image to that of Demeas: both comment on the absence of the groom, but whereas Demeas was calm and soothing, Nikeratos restores the comic atmosphere that allows the play to draw to its end.

718. I'll arrest you on the spot: In the context of his charge of seduction – the strongest denunciation of Moschion in the whole play (cf. 612 n.) – Nikeratos' intention is doubtless to force marriage on the young man as the penalty for his actions (Harrison p. 19). The seriousness of the threat, however, is largely defused by its patently otiose nature at this stage in the action, except as the vehicle for a final display of bluster that restores the initiative to Moschion and allows him once more to avoid the embarrassment of a climb-down. By threatening arrest, Nikeratos provides the cue for a display of histrionic resistance from the young man. This in turn obliges Nikeratos and Demeas to resort to appeals in order to calm the situation, appeals which significantly provide the form if not the substance of what Moschion wanted at 665ff. (Are Moschion's virtual invitations to be arrested at 719 and 722 ironic, as most editors suppose, or a sign that he would welcome it as a way out of the need to explain away his appearance or apologise for his actions?) Able therefore to pretend – to himself at least – that he submits as a favour rather than because he has to, Moschion can now claim the paper victory he had earlier hoped for (cf. Sandbach[1], W.S. Anderson[2] p. 160), a victory that echoes in some respects Sostratos' ironic claim at *Old Cantankerous* 864f. to have achieved his betrothal by his own efforts.

727. And as dowry...when I die: The conversion of the usual dowry into inheritance fulfils a twofold function. Logically it may be interpreted as in keeping with the lack of capital that seems to have been a feature of Nikeratos throughout the action. More importantly, perhaps, it marks a final comic intervention from the old man with overtones of both the conventional love match which needs no dowry (cf. *Old Cantankerous* 307f.) and the dowryless marriage that a rapist could be forced to accept.

730. Chrysis: This final, almost incidental, mention of Chrysis serves in fact: (1) to bring back to the audience's attention a character who has the title role of the play but has been altogether absent since 575, and to include her in the wedding celebrations as Moschion wanted, and (2) to signal by the instruction for her to send out the other members of Demeas' household the fact that she has returned to that position of authority she occupied when the play began. In this way Menander economically suggests a resumption of the couple's earlier relationship without the need for any overt reference or the development of a sub-plot that might have detracted from the main focus of interest – father and son (cf. Goldberg[2] p. 106, Fantham p. 66).

The reintroduction of Chrysis has also raised for some commentators the question of the baby's own fate: will it now return to its natural parents or will it continue to be reared by Chrysis? This latter course is advocated by Keuls[2] p. 18 and supported by Sandbach[2] who argues (1) that nothing is said at 77-9 to suggest that the baby's status will be affected by the marriage of Moschion and Plangon – there is no implication of Chrysis keeping it only for the time being; (2) that Moschion gives no sign of wishing to assume responsibility for it even after Demeas declares he is in favour of a marriage between the young couple; and (3) that the alternative scenario – revealing the child's true origins only after the marriage – would indicate to Demeas he had been deceived by both his mistress and his son. To each of these a counter-argument might readily be found.

More important, however, is the absolute silence of Menander on the matter, suggesting either that he had no dramatic interest in the child's subsequent history and did not expect any from his audience, or that he relied upon the audience reaching what he felt to be a conclusion self-evident at the time, if less so to ourselves. The most objective source of possible information on the situation presented, the records of court cases, is altogether lacking in analogies. We are thrown back, therefore, onto other potential sources. One of these is Menander himself; for in *The Arbitration*, also founded upon pre-marital rape, the slave Onesimos describes the danger of divorce faced by his mistress Pamphile if her husband Charisios, suspected of fathering the foundling in question, discovers the identity of its mother (568ff.). The basis of such a scenario is the presumption that a subsequent marriage between Charisios and the mother would legitimise the baby, which effectively cuts across the arguments of those who would leave Moschion's child in a state of legal limbo. A further factor to be taken into consideration is natural justice, which plays an important role in the dénouement of many Menandrean plays. In the view of Keuls and Sandbach the child would continue to live in Demeas' house, the marital home also of Moschion and Plangon, but would not be acknowledged by them. That this would be contrary to natural justice needs no demonstration. Rather, what Menander has done in depicting the return of the infant to Demeas' house at 575 is in fact to inject an unspoken suggestion of its restoration to its rightful place in preparation for the marriage of its parents, just as the similar return of Chrysis presupposes, without the need for any direct reference, the restoration of her own relationship to Demeas (see further Dedoussi).

734ff. Pretty boys...: On the formulaic ending of the play with its torches, garlands and appeals for audience favour see *Old Cantankerous*.

The Arbitration

Act I

Before the fragmentary remains of Act I, which commence with Smikrines' complaints about Charisios' drinking habits (127), editors have
traditionally inserted a number of shorter passages culled from the works
of other ancient writers. The first four of these in the translation indicate
that the play's original opening scene was predictably expository, establishing both the antecedents of the action portrayed and the characters
involved in it, principally Onesimos, whose inquisitiveness has led to the
break-up of his master's marriage. The fifth fragment, in contrast, may be
better associated with the third scene of the play, preparing the way for
Smikrines' references to Charisios' profligacy after he left home and
moved in with his friend Chairestratos. The fact that Chairestratos himself is able to comment on the old man's outbursts by means of asides
suggests that he too had been on stage for some time before the extant
text begins and had withdrawn to one side at the appearance of Smikrines, as Chrysis does at *The Girl From Samos* 59. In between these two
scenes commentators have rightly supposed the existence of a deferred
prologue delivered by a divine figure, as in *The Shield*, which would have
provided that one factor upon which the widespread development of
dramatic irony is based: the true origins of the child.

127. he's drinking very expensive wine!: An early instance of the
dramatic irony in the play. Smikrines' interpretation of his son-in-law's
behaviour is based on the logical, though inaccurate, belief that Charisios
has simply lapsed into unbridled hedonism. Through the intervention of
the divine prologue, on the other hand, the audience would by now be
aware that its cause is really an attempt to drown his sorrows after the
shock of recent events. Indeed, much of the pathos built into the action
derives from the audience's realisation that Charisios' behaviour harms
himself no less than it does his wife. True, in terms of modern morality,
his behaviour towards Pamphile since discovering that she was not a

63

virgin at the time of their marriage and has given birth to a seemingly illegitimate child, smacks of double standards, especially in view of his own pre-marital rape. But in terms of ancient values, and the situation as he understands it, his reaction is a far cry from the repudiation of Pamphile required by the law (cf. Harrison p. 35f., Sandbach[1] p. 292). What Menander suggests, in fact, is not that Charisios has ever ceased to love his wife, but that something has come between them which threatens to drive them irrevocably apart: the pregnancy. Once it is shown that the child's illegitimacy is an illusion, their reconciliation is as reasonable an assumption as it was in the case of Demeas and Chrysis in *The Girl from Samos* or Pamphilus and Philumena in Terence's *The Mother-in-Law* (see further Ireland[2] p. 13ff.).

132f. break up the party: The reference is doubtless to Charisios' carousing with Habrotonon, which Chairestratos, like Smikrines, interprets at face value. Only at 430ff. in the extant text does Menander make clear through Habrotonon that her employer will have nothing to do with her, thereby adding further confirmation of the young man's emotional turmoil.

133. But that's.... Damn him!: Attribution of the line is disputed. Many assign it to Chairestratos, his rejection of any personal involvement in the situation. This would then allow continuation of the old man's fixation with money: from the complaints of how much Charisios is spending on wine to thoughts of the dowry he gained and which he is now ostensibly squandering (cf. Arnott[4] *ad loc.*). Others assign it to Smikrines, arguing that it allows a shift of emphasis away from purely financial considerations to the quality of Charisios' behaviour towards his wife, even if the old man chooses to represent the neglect Pamphile is suffering in terms that are rooted in finance. In either case the effect is ultimately the same – the portrayal of Smikrines as tight-fisted.

134. a large dowry: lit. four talents (24,000 drachmas) compared with one and three talents in *Old Cantankerous* (844f.) cf. *The Rape of the Locks* (1015), and two talents in *The Shield* (135) and *The Man She Hated* (446). At first sight the size of the dowry seems out of proportion to Smikrines' evident parsimony, but it may serve to suggest a greater obligation on the husband to avoid marital difficulties (see further *Old Cantankerous* 308 n.). Certainly, when developed for its comic potential, the theme of a rich wife reducing her husband to a subservient position was something of a commonplace: Anaxandrides fr. 52 'A man who is poor and takes a wife with money gets a tyrant not a wife', Menander fr. 333 'To think that I married Krobule with a dowry of sixteen talents and a nose a foot long! How can I stand her unbearable airs?', fr. 334 'I have an heiress Vampire as wife. Didn't I tell you? - No. – She's the mistress of my house and lands...', Plautus' *The Pot of Gold* 498ff. As a result, questions of whether the size of such dowries represented contemporary reality become otiose in comparison to their dramatic value. It may well be, as Arnott[4] suggests on *Old Cantankerous* 740, that their size signalled not absolute values but the relative prosperity of families.

136f. £20 a day: lit. 12 drachmas, which, at the rate of 50 pence a day (lit. 2 obols = $^1/_3$ drachma) mentioned by Chairestratos in 140, would last 36 days, and had in fact been the subsidy paid to a poor man and his wife in the period of the Peloponnesian war a hundred years before. Smikrines' reference therefore would seem to indicate further his obsession with penny-pinching finance.

to a pimp: Menander introduces at this relatively early stage the fact that unlike many of the more attractive *hetairai* of New Comedy (Chrysis in the *Girl from Samos*, Thais in Terence's *The Eunuch* and Bacchis in *The Mother-in-Law*) Habrotonon is not a free agent but a slave in the control of a pimp. This, in some respects, serves to explain the element of self-interest that colours her later intervention in the action and increases the reality of her portrayal.

142. Habrotonon: Though the text nowhere identifies by name or reference the character who appears at this point (which itself suggests she has already appeared on stage in one of the missing sections of the play), the fact that she clearly emerges from Chairestratos' house, has ostensibly been sent by Charisios, and uses the familiar 'darling' makes it virtually inevitable that we assign the part to Habrotonon.

159f. Bless you...like that: Damage to the text makes interpretation of the action less than totally certain. A likely scenario would be for Smikrines to become aware of the other two, intervene angrily in their dialogue and thus provoke the reaction of 159.

167. The one next door: Why should Habrotonon want Chairestratos' house turned upside down? The suggestion that her profession requires husbands to be unhappy and to turn to women like herself seems hardly appropriate in the circumstances, since Charisios is already in just such a state. More likely, perhaps, she here foreshadows the neglect her employer displays towards her (432ff.) – something that may have figured in the prologue – suggesting the need for his attitude to be shaken up and his behaviour towards her to come more into line with expectations.

169. a bunch of young drunks: The conventional introduction of the chorus at the end of the first Act, cf. *Old Cantankerous, The Rape of the Locks, The Shield.*

Act II

218. You're trying …decent thing: This is either the opening line of the dialogue between the two slaves as they enter (since it was often Menander's practice to introduce characters as if in mid-conversation, cf. *Old Cantankerous* 50ff., 233ff., 430ff.), or close to it, since the overall effect is the same. Editors differ in detail as regards attribution of individual statements here, but the consequences of resulting variations are unimportant.

And…blackmail me: cf. *The Girl from Samos* 575 n.

219. You've no right to keep what's not yours: Though we can hardly doubt that the audience was immediately able to infer the cause of the dispute, both as a result of the expository prologue and from the presence on stage of a baby and a bag suitable for containing trinkets, Menander appears to tantalise by studiously avoiding any overt reference to the baby itself in the extant text until Daos begins to state his case at 240ff. Instead, his statements here, at 222 ('cut you in') and at 237 ('offer him a deal') establish the basis of the dispute without the substance.

222f. Will you accept him as arbitrator?: The use of unofficial arbitration to settle disputes was common in Athens, especially where the point at issue involved natural justice rather than statute law, and its findings were legally binding on both parties so long as they had agreed beforehand to accept the arbitrator and the judgement made (cf. Plautus' *The Rope* 1035ff., which contains the additional comic element of Gripus deceitfully obtaining his own master as arbitrator – only to come off worse in the end).

227. someone impartial: Though an essential functional component of any arbitration, Menander's insertion of the phrase underlines the irony of Smikrines' role here – a grandfather unwittingly sitting in judgement on the fate of his own grandson – an irony further emphasised by Syros introducing the matter as subject to the old man's convenience.

229. Traipsing about in overalls: lit. the *diphthera* or leather jerkin, which figured as a sign of rural life in the dream Sostratos' mother had in *Old Cantankerous* 407ff.

239. You start: Why has Menander chosen to reverse normal legal procedure and to make Daos, the defendant, state his case first? To Sandbach[1] the answer lies in dramatic and oratorical effectiveness: the greater rhetorical persuasiveness of Syros' speech virtually demands the more important second position and allows him to rebut his opponent's arguments all the more forcibly. The fact that Smikrines invites Daos to speak first suggests indeed his tacit support for the slave, the reverse of the hostility he has demonstrated towards Syros from the outset. Syros it was, after all, who first approached the old man and requested arbitration, Syros who in consequence became the butt of Smikrines' irritation at the private wrangling of two slaves, who was forced as a result into a display of increasing deference (230ff.) and hence into a position of weakness, and who continues to provoke the old man's indignation right up to 293. That it is Syros who nevertheless wins the day is an undeniable vindication of the stand he takes.

245. I found a little new-born baby: The exposure of infants for reasons of poverty, illegitimacy, or simply being the wrong sex (i.e., female) where they might be found and reared by others, if they survived at all, was a frequent enough motif in ancient drama, both tragedy (e.g., Euripides' *Ion*) and comedy, to need no further explanation. Similarly, the mention of trinkets found with it was a conventional device by which the child's identity might later be established (see further 455ff.).

250ff.: As Goldberg[2] p. 66 observes, in formulating the speeches, Menander places as much emphasis upon delineating the characters of the two slaves through the way in which they present their arguments, as on the arguments themselves. So it is that for all the ostensible primacy of Daos' case in terms of his initial discovery of the child and its trinkets, his claim is constantly undermined by a series of subtle self-revelations that demonstrate his inherent unworthiness: (1) his almost total absorption with self, shown by the constant reference to his own viewpoint (250-6), (2) his second thoughts (252ff.), suggestive of inconstancy and unreliability; and (3) his description of rearing the child as bothersome and expensive (254f.), an undertaking to make him 'down-in-the-mouth' (260). To these character indicators we might add other factors that weaken the slave's case structurally by breaking the thread of his argument: his inability to distinguish what is relevant from what is not, his tendency to insert material as it occurs to him irrespective of its usefulness – the obtrusive parenthesis 'he's a charcoal burner, I've known him for years' (257f.), for instance – and the extended direct quotations inserted into his account.

In contrast, Syros' speech is both shrewd and carefully structured. It begins with an admission of his opponent's accuracy where this cannot be avoided and where it will not damage his own case. It seeks to refute not by subtraction but by addition, suggesting that Daos' apparently full account omitted some highly salient details. It studiously avoids any imputation of claiming the trinkets for self-advantage or out of greed by representing Syros as motivated by an altruistic desire to be the child's champion (306f., 315ff.), not his pillager, as Daos by implication must inevitably appear (312f.). It appeals to the support of Smikrines through the flattering reference to the old man's knowledge of the mythological analogies Syros introduces (325ff.). Finally, it counters Daos' earlier insistence that the child be handed back to him if Syros is no longer willing to abide by the initial agreement (289f.) by extending Daos' view of rearing it as 'bothersome' to its natural conclusion in scarcely veiled hints of total despoliation (348-51).

270. You admit…I do: The line is disputed in terms of both text and attribution of parts. The evidence of the papyrus, where Smikrines' name occurs in the margin, suggests 'You admit…Syros' be given to the old man. This seems unlikely, however, since (1) there is no evidence that Smikrines knows Syros' name at this point in the action – indeed the whole basis of the episode is that Smikrines is dealing with total strangers; and (2) the normally adopted supplement 'I do', inserted after the question to restore the line to its proper length, would divide it unusually between three speakers. The most reasonable remedy, therefore, suggests either (1) reassigning the question to Daos (as in the translation), which Sandbach[1] argues would be typical of the slave's tendency to emphasise the inessential (cf. 275), or (2) emendation of the line by omitting the name Syros and altering the supplement as Arnott[4] suggests: '*Smikrines*: Did you ask? *Daos*: He spent the whole day ‹pleading›…'.

my dear friend Syros?: The only location in the extant text where the slave's name occurs, and even then it is in the diminutive form Syriskos, normally indicative of sympathetic contact, but here used with clearly sarcastic overtones; hence the translation's 'my dear friend'. Some, however, have suggested Syriskos is the slave's real name, despite the evidence of the Mytilene mosaic (see Turner[1] Pl.1,B) where the form given is Syros (CYPOC).

276f. trashy bits…not worth anything: By depreciating the value of the trinkets Daos attempts to minimise their importance and consequently to belittle Syros' case as straining after a gnat. In doing so, however, he unwittingly also weakens the force of his own claim; for if they are of such small value, why does he prove so reluctant to give them up? In much the same way his insistence that Syros should be grateful for what he got (280) is directly undercut by the description of Syros' reaction on receiving the child (272ff.) and pointedly reveals Daos as reducing the dispute to considerations of pure finance, not justice.

293. Has he finished?: How are we to interpret the question? Suggestions that Syros attempts to ensure Daos has finished so as to avoid the punishment Smikrines threatened at 248f. seem unlikely, since he has already intervened twice in response to Daos' questions. The irony inherent in such a question, moreover, would prove counter-productive in a situation where Syros depends upon securing Smikrines' good will. More likely, therefore, the question marks an initial diminution of Daos' case by the oblique observation that it contains little of any substance if this is all it amounts to.

299. A shepherd that he talked to: The first point of addition to Daos' account (see 250ff. n.), a seemingly unimportant item but enough to suggest his description of events was not without significant omissions: his failure, for instance, to reveal from the outset that trinkets were found with the baby. Similarly, compared to Daos' earlier description of the trinkets as 'trashy bits', Syros' readiness to suggest they may be gold (309) and his very frankness in the context of Daos' insinuations of self-interest, serve to suggest it is he who is the more trustworthy of the two.

302f. Give me the child, dear: Syros' introduction of the baby physically into the proceedings – especially significant for an audience that knows its relationship to Smikrines – and the emphasis he places upon his role as no more than mouthpiece (cf. 316f. 'I am asking absolutely nothing for myself') set Daos' actions in a less than favourable light, particularly the slave's restriction of the dispute to himself and Syros at 289ff. The contrast between the attitudes of the two slaves is further compounded by the dichotomy that surrounds both the trinkets' function: 'they were put there for his adornment, not to keep you in food' (305), and the intentions of the giver and finder: 'should the trinkets...be kept for the baby...that's why his mother...gave them to him? Or should the thief keep them...?' (309-12).

307. your gift: Though Syros has been careful to emphasise the fact that the claim to the trinkets comes primarily from the baby, he must also justify his own involvement as spokesman for the child and rebut Daos' charge that the disputed objects are none of his concern. Significantly the two are achieved by Daos' own actions in transferring guardianship of the child to Syros.

313. Why, you may ask...: As Sandbach[1] observes, Syros puts into Daos' mouth a question he never asked. He then proceeds to answer it not with logic – because at the time he was unaware of the trinkets' existence – but with a reply that is illogical in view of 306f. ('for I'm...made me that'), but is calculated to appeal to pathos and thus more likely to hit home. In much the same way Syros' reference in 317 to 'sharing the lucky find' echoes but also twists Daos' use of the phrase at 284, where it was introduced specifically to claim what he had *not* done. Syros then strengthens the effect of his argument with the jingle established in the Greek of 319 'It's not a find; it's more like robbing blind'.

324. lion-hunting: Deliberately fanciful, but by exploiting the gulf that may separate the slaves from the baby, the idea is designed to appeal to Smikrines' sense of justice, and is backed by the flattery that represents him as a cultured expert on the tragic theatre and its plots.

328. an old goatherd, dressed just like me: By associating himself with the character of the myth in terms of dress, Syros implies a similar link between his own championing of the child and the behaviour of the goatherd. In contrast, the introduction of Daos at 334ff. 'Now, if Daos had taken those tokens...' shows by reverse analogy the danger his opponent represents to the baby's future welfare for the sake of literally twelve drachmas, the same as can be used to hire Habrotonon for a day (136f.).

343ff. Nature...of doing so: A sententious finale to the theme of unresolved identity before Syros turns to rebut the final point in Daos' argument, 'Hand the baby back...', inserted with an abruptness calculated to suggest there is no reasoning behind it, only self-interest.

358-75. That's a terrible verdict...: Daos' reaction to the verdict – the extent to which his sense of aggrieved disappointment is developed and the language in which it is expressed – serves to restore a more comic atmosphere after the relative formality of the arbitration (cf. Gripus' reaction to his own loss in Plautus' *The Rope*, Goldberg[2] p. 67f.).

381. let's go over them: The cue for Syros and his wife to go into a huddle, which neatly prepares for the shift of attention to Onesimos when he appears, his involvement in identifying the ring, and through this the return of Charisios into dramatic focus.

387. What's going on here?: Onesimos' intervention has already been prepared for by his tendency to be 'nosey', referred to in the second fragment at the opening of the play.

391. And who are you?: The fact that Syros' question receives no reply signals the virtual end of his role in the play. For all his prominence in the Arbitration scene he progressively loses control of the situation, as he fails to regain possession of the ring once Onesimos has seized it, despite all his protestations (reminiscent of those so recently heard from Daos) and his repetition of the baby's claim, a claim that had proved so decisive to his own acquisition of it. Ironically, however, it is Syros' intervention at the beginning of Act III that initiates a similar diminution of Onesimos' own role when in the course of their argument he induces Onesimos to reveal the circumstances of the ring's loss. One result of this is to attract the attention of Habrotonon and to bring about her intervention in the situation, and since Onesimos' unpopularity with his master already severely limits his room for manoeuvre, it then prompts him to hand over to the music girl responsibility for resolving both the ring's ownership and the whole question of the baby's true origins.

Act III

The usual bridging of Acts by means of character and theme (the ring – significantly the first words in the Greek) is here augmented by the appearance of Onesimos and Habrotonon from Chairestratos' house, both eager to escape a difficult situation inside, both preoccupied by thoughts of Charisios, and brought together by Syros. Onesimos' opening speech itself fulfils a twofold role:

1) It underlines the problems that beset him from every side (a potential contrast in Blundell's view, p. 28, to the self-satisfaction that may have marked his role in Act I) and thus provides motivation for the prominence of Habrotonon in the rest of the play.

2) It signals a shift in the portrayal of Charisios: from outrage at Pamphile's supposed behaviour to anger at Onesimos as the source of information, which explains the slave's reluctance to fulfil the role again. Likewise, Habrotonon's own description of Charisios, pointedly rejecting any sexual relationship with her, contrasts strongly with the picture earlier painted by Smikrines (see below 437 n.), but is itself soon balanced by the observation that he may also be the perpetrator of rape (447ff.).

Though the connection between Acts II and III is clear enough in terms of structure and theme, commentators remain divided over whether the time-interval represented by the choral interlude signals the passage of a whole night or merely separates two parts of the same day. The former view is largely founded on (1) the mention of 'tomorrow' by both Onesimos (414) and Syros (379, 415); (2) the agitation of Syros at learning Onesimos has not yet shown the ring to Charisios as he promised (442ff.); (3) references to the duration of the party alluded to by Onesimos (383) and Habrotonon (440); and (4) the consequent increase in realism to be gained from spreading over two days the crowded activity of the play (Sandbach[1] p. 325f.[2]). The latter, more frequently advanced, view derives mainly from: (1) the general convention of New Comedy plots taking place within the space of a single day; (2) the mention by Onesimos of having acquired the ring 'just now' (436); (3) the resulting difficulty of explaining Syros' movements in Act III in the light of his statement at 379ff. that he and his wife will go back to work the next day; (4) the problem of Habrotonon's entry at 430 being set at the beginning of a new day; and (5) the possibility of Onesimos' reference to 'tomorrow' (414) being intended simply as prevarication (cf. Arnott[8]).

429. the present stew's quite bad enough: For Onesimos every scenario he can envisage, both real and imagined, holds out the prospect of disaster. Already he has had to suffer Charisios' hostility for revealing Pamphile's disgrace. If he carries out his intention of showing the ring, he introduces the suggestion of a link between his master and an illegitimate child, a suggestion which 457 ('Without her evidence...suspicion and chaos') indicates he has no means of substantiating. And even if the rupture in relations between husband and wife is healed – at this stage a hypothetical rather than real possibility – he remains the embarrassing possessor of information both master and mistress would rather forget, and liable in consequence to be put out of the way.

430ff. Let me go, please! Leave me alone!: The plural verbs in the Greek reveal the cause of Habrotonon's appearance: a desire to escape the attentions of other young men at Charisios' party, whose behaviour towards her contrasts strikingly with the neglect she experiences from Charisios himself.

433. the man positively hates me: Oblique confirmation of Charisios' continuing love for Pamphile already implicit in Onesimos' previous statement and developed with greater force in Act IV. For all his ostensible harshness towards Pamphile, Charisios shows no signs of enjoying the supposedly riotous lifestyle earlier reported; instead it takes on the guise of a desperate attempt – all too unsuccessful – to drown his sorrows, and as such helps to retain some vestige of audience sympathy for him (cf. Polemon's actions in *The Rape of the Locks*).

437. Why is he wasting all this money?: The question is an ironic echo of Smikrines' complaint in Act I, but whereas the old man had envisaged the active squandering of money on high living, Habrotonon reveals that the expenses have been incurred to no purpose. The observation also initiates a subtle characterisation of Habrotonon as someone prone to view things in financial terms. In her later description of the rape, for instance, beauty and wealth stand side by side as the girl's foremost characteristics (484f.); the effects of the rape are characterised as much by the ruin of the girl's fine clothing as by the emotional turmoil created in her (487ff.); the alternative scenarios envisaged for the loss of Charisios' ring (502-6) all involve some form of financial basis; even the gratitude she envisages may come from establishing the baby's true parentage is not without its hope of freedom purchased (549). In this way Menander establishes a character who, while capable of generous actions, retains a degree of self-interest that makes her human and engaging (see further 464 n.).

442. Syros: For all its intrinsic interest the re-entry of the slave and his interaction with Onesimos are determined principally by technical considerations. Through it Menander establishes the significance of the ring as a link between Charisios, the baby, the Tauropolia and potential rape. By its vehemence it attracts the attention of Habrotonon, allowing confirmation of the connection between festival and rape, and then motivates her assumption of responsibility for effecting the dénouement.

453. a girl got raped: See *The Girl from Samos* 49n.

455f. find the girl and produce the ring: Menander neatly introduces the convention of a raped girl seizing some article from her assailant by which his identity might later be established or which could be left with any resulting baby, if it was exposed, as a token of its origins. The seriousness of the act imputed to Charisios is mitigated in stage terms, however, by the as yet unknown identity of the victim and by the audience's knowledge that Charisios has already made some partial reparation for his crime by marrying his victim (contrast Terence's *The Mother-in-Law*).

460f. Going shares isn't my line: An echo of the arbitration scene where Syros had similarly rejected any idea of dividing the baby's property (317).

464. the baby: In contrast to Onesimos' concentration upon the ring, the very first words of Habrotonon's intervention (in the Greek text) set the child firmly at the centre of her concern, a concern already foreshadowed by the sympathy shown for Charisios, and which forms the true foundation of her subsequent involvement. Only later does the element of possible self-advantage emerge (540ff.), introduced significantly by Onesimos once the scheme to establish the baby's identity has been formulated (cf. Arnott[5] p. 354f.).

472. he was drunk and disorderly: See *The Girl from Samos* 328 n.

475. I saw it: The essential element of coincidence that enables resolution of a plot itself founded on the coincidental marriage of rapist and victim, and a prominent feature of New Comedy in general.

479. I was still a virgin: The statement demonstrates Menander's ability to introduce elements of subtle characterisation, in this case Habrotonon's tendency to empathise with the disadvantaged. Already she has shown her concern to prevent Charisios' child being reared as a slave, like herself, for want of recognition; now recollection of the rape that occured at the Tauropolia brings back memories of her own lost virginity, a loss which can have been no more her own choice as a slave in the power of a pimp than it was for Pamphile.

483f. I'd know her if I saw her: This is the most obvious way of discovering the girl's identity and, in the event, it is the method actually employed. As a result it produces a relatively rapid and easy resolution of the plot, but only after Menander has fully exploited those complicating themes already introduced and which are the main interest of the action: Charisios and Smikrines. For the time being therefore the question of the rape-victim's identity is forced into the background, since as yet there is nothing to connect the girl with either the ring or the baby.

495. If the mother's a girl of good family: Habrotonon's observation hints at a scenario expressed in more transparent terms by Onesimos at 568ff.: divorce of Pamphile, from whom Charisios is ostensibly estranged, in order to marry the child's mother and thus gain the son and heir every Greek male wanted. From the audience's viewpoint, of course, the suggestion is packed with irony.

497f. let's find out who she *is*: In the context of Habrotonon's proposed course of action Onesimos' interruption is clearly motivated by the same thoughts of self-preservation as opened the Act. Rejection of his alternative plan on the other hand now signals the shift in control of the situation to Habrotonon. To her feminine instincts confirmation of Charisios' paternity takes precedence over awakening the girl's disgrace, which she has already attempted to cover by abandoning the baby.

515. Go on...: Like 'Clever girl!' (520), 'Super!' (525), 'Great!' (528), 'You're a genius !' (532), 'You're a minx...one' (535), the interjections serve to break up the details of Habrotonon's plan, enlivening the various phases of its revelation, facilitating the audience's grasp of it, and steering its reaction to what she proposes in the direction Menander desires (cf. *Old Cantankerous* 102-17, *The Shield* Act I). Similarly, the description of the plan itself is made all the more vivid by the use of direct speech and the proposed manipulation of Charisios' reactions, natural to someone in Habrotonon's profession.

532. ask the woman: Daos' wife, who had earlier entered Chairestratos' house. In this way, having used the ring to establish the link between Charisios and the rape, Habrotonon can then extend the link to include the baby.

541. But it would be nice if he did: As suggested in 464 n., self-interest only emerges once genuine concern for the baby and its mother have been established. Why though is it introduced at all? The answer lies probably in the playwright's wish to make Habrotonon a fully humanised character (cf. 437 n.), one whose servile status and profession would make totally disinterested concern unnatural. At the same time Menander is careful to limit thoughts of personal advantage by specifically exploring its extent. By raising and then rejecting the possibility of Habrotonon seeking further advantage through abandonment of the search for the child's real mother (544ff.) and thus perpetuating the fiction she here envisages, Menander avoids potential problems of his own making. He creates a fully credible character while minimising the fault that brings about that credibility, showing Habrotonon in no way anxious to take on responsibility for rearing a child, and backing this up with Onesimos' own warning should she change her mind.

555. Sweet Persuasion: Peitho, goddess of both oratorical and erotic persuasion. In view of references to Pan in the course of *Old Cantankerous* and to Chance in *The Shield* it may not be altogether otiose to see in the mention of Persuasion here a reference to the speaker of *The Arbitration*'s lost prologue.

557ff. Onesimos: Technically this is an exit monologue designed to round off the scene and to introduce the arrival of Smikrines. In dramatic terms on the other hand it reinforces what Arnott[5] p. 355 describes as cross-characterisation; for whereas it is normally the male slave in New Comedy who displays ingenuity in devising and employing strategems (e.g., Daos in *The Shield*), here it is a woman who assumes the role while Onesimos can only stand by helpless: 'So what does a man do?' (511), 'But me...drivelling and paralytic, quite incapable of a scheme like this.' (560ff.). At the same time his apprehension for his mistress' future maintains an element of tension which both balances the optimism of Habrotonon's plan and injects an element of dramatic irony for an audience aware of how groundless his fears are.

573. none of *my* stirring: At the end of the scene Onesimos shows clear relief that any trouble arising from Habrotonon's scheme will not rebound onto him, unlike his earlier intervention in the situation described at the beginning of the Act.

580ff. Better go before he sees me: As the translation indicates, Onesimos' exit is followed by scenes that are highly fragmentary and of which only a bare outline is possible. Detailed consideration of the extant tatters, together with a speculative restoration, is provided by Arnott[4] (cf. Frost p. 72f.). Clearly, events in Act IV require Smikrines to learn of the supposed relationship between Charisios and Habrotonon, hence the relevance of the remains at 645f., addressed in all probability to Chairestratos: 'This companion of yours (Charisios) wasn't ashamed to father a baby on a whore', and his determination to remove his daughter at 657. The immediate seriousness of such a discovery, however, was doubtless diminished by the presence on stage for part of the time of the cook Karion complaining incongruously at the loss of a hiring (611ff.): 'I'm totally out of luck. For some reason the party's breaking up, but if anyone happens (to need) a cook...you can go to blazes' and by the audience's superior knowledge, which reduces the old man's annoyance to the ridiculous. Following this Smikrines must have exited into Charisios' house in an attempt to persuade his daughter to leave her marital home.

Act IV

In the tradition of Greek New Comedy, in so far as the plays of Menander allow us to establish a tradition, the fourth Act sees development of the plot's major crisis and its subsequent resolution. In the present instance this is extended to development of a double crisis, one involving both husband and wife in separately presented, though interrelated and equally unwelcome, difficulties. However, it is significant that although the plot centres upon Charisios and Pamphile, neither has as yet appeared on stage, instead being represented thus far by surrogates. Their inclusion in Act IV, therefore, becomes increasingly effective in dramatic terms as each in turn is brought face to face with the implications of the situation in which they are embroiled. In Pamphile's case the crisis that surrounds her is engineered by her own father: his attempt to break up her marriage (foreshadowed at the end of Act III) by portraying the impossibility of a relationship complicated by a mistress – in itself an ironic scenario built upon misapprehension. Despite the defence of her marriage which Pamphile makes, a spirited defence to judge from subsequently discovered fragments of their dialogue (*Oxyrhynchus Papyri* 3532-3), the reported snatches at 920ff. (cf. Papyrus Didot I, translation p. 250f.) and its effect upon Charisios, she is nevertheless powerless to prevent the awakening of fresh misery. The result is an enormous injection of pathos and sympathy, which positively demand the intervention of Habrotonon to pluck her from the depths of undeserved despair.

Rescuing Charisios from his own predicament is, in contrast, a more straight-forward task once the relationship between Pamphile and the baby is established. His responsibility for the situation on the other hand, the initial rape followed by desertion of his wife because of a disgrace the audience knows he has himself caused, requires express demonstration that he is worthy of rescue before it is thrust into his lap. Already an element of audience sympathy for him has been aroused by his use of high-living in a vain attempt to blot out from his mind the misery of a rejected wife. Now in Act IV his reaction to Pamphile's loyalty and the self-knowledge he gains in consequence serve to display the contrition necessary for his future happiness.

749. Just think what that would cost!: As earlier in the play, Smikrines' arguments gravitate to considerations of finance, described by Sandbach[1] as 'the characteristic pettiness of his calculations'.

the women's festivals: lit. the Thesmophoria, held over three days in the autumn to celebrate the fruits provided by the goddess Demeter, and the Skira, a one-day festival in the summer, likewise dedicated to Demeter. Ironically, it may have been at just such a festival that Pamphile was raped (cf. the Adonis festival in *The Girl from Samos*).

752. the harbour: lit. the Piraeus, the harbour of Athens where Smikrines envisages Charisios installing his mistress – away from the town house and his wife, but accessible whenever he felt the need.

856. when will you see your mother?: A pointedly ironic instance of foreshadowing just before the point of recognition. Menander's arrangement of this displays in fact considerable sophistication, in particular the shifting reactions of the two women to one another (Sandbach[1] p. 359).

76

Habrotonon's formal use of 'madam' at 858, for instance, is the natural result of a desire to attract attention while avoiding the hostile response that might be expected in view of her profession. Once she recognises Pamphile, she easily lapses into the more relaxed 'darling' and 'sweet-heart' of 860 and 862. Such familiarity, however, is unmatched by Pamphile herself, who is unaware of its cause and is forced by Habrotonon's apparent forwardness into maintaining the social divide that separates them by her own use of 'madam' at 859 and 864. The latter of these, set in the important position of first word in its line and sentence (unprecedented in Menander), also signals a shift to the girl as controller of the dialogue. By failing to respond to Habrotonon's question in the previous line and posing one of her own instead, Pamphile induces Habrotonon, conscious that her investigations are beginning to bear fruit (hence the 'love' of 865), nevertheless to return to formal address in 866 in a determined effort to maintain contact in the face of Pamphile's evident astonishment. Ironically, once the realisation of the truth emerges, it is Pamphile who assumes the less formal style with 'my dear' (871, lit. 'darling' as in 860) while Habrotonon maintains the formality due to a respectable married woman (873).

883ff. You see...: Just as the process of rescuing Pamphile from her difficulties was preceded by a demonstration of her wifely virtue, so rehabilitation of Charisios through self-criticism precedes his own salvation. The importance of the young man's growth in self-knowledge is emphasised indeed by the scale of its presentation and by the use of two sources for this purpose – speeches in turn from Onesimos and Charisios. This allows not only the introduction of variety but also the possibility of pointing emphases through contrast and verbal echo. The two speeches are contrasted, for instance, in that the one from Onesimos is clearly inserted for the benefit of the audience, hence the purely narrative element of explaining Charisios' eavesdropping, the use of clarifying statements such as 'My master, I mean, Charisios' (880) and the direct reference to the audience in 887. Charisios' speech, on the other hand, exhibits all the self-absorption of the true soliloquy with a consequent gain in emotional intensity. Similarly, though both speeches contain direct quotation, there is a definite increase in force between one and the other: from Charisios' criticism of his heartless action towards Pamphile (890ff.) to the more sombre, biting, quasi-objective criticism of the imagined deity, further strengthened by Pamphile's pointedly generous defence of her husband. Verbal echoes between the speeches on the other hand come most obviously from the use of the same root-word in the Greek to link the fortunes of husband and wife: 'mess' (891), 'victim' (898), 'bad luck' (914), 'unfortunate' (918), and from the repetition of 'brute' in 898 and as an isolated word in the lacuna at 924 (the apparent

echo in 918 of the translation does not occur in the original; see further
Blundell p. 34f.).

inside the door here: i.e., inside Chairestratos' house listening to the
dialogue on stage between Smikrines and his daughter.

895ff. *I* behave like this...similar outrage: Like 914ff. the observation
underlines the dichotomy between Charisios' and Pamphile's situations: Charisios the agent of rape, Pamphile the victim who suffers
further as a result rather than attracting sympathy. This highlights in fact
the deep division between male and female sexual morality in ancient
society. For the male, extra-marital affairs with *hetairai* did not constitute
adultery and the offspring of such liaisons posed no threat to the family
unit since they had no automatic right of inheritance and no right at all to
citizen status. Even Smikrines' anger at his son-in-law's behaviour is
pointedly financial, not moral. For a wife on the other hand, whose
function was to bear legitimate children, fidelity was paramount. How
though would the audience have viewed Charisios' attitude here? In
absolute terms, his self-criticism may have seemed decidedly advanced
thinking in the context of a sullied wife, who could expect little more
than automatic repudiation. This would be balanced, however, by the
realisation that Charisios' behaviour is justified by the unusual circumstances: a young man's reaction to a rape that we know was his own
doing.

930. My wife's not leaving me: How are we to interpret Charisios'
statement here? Clearly not as a decision to return to his wife despite his
continuing love for her, since it responds solely to the immediate situation, the difficulties posed by Smikrines. It does nothing to address the
real problem faced by the marriage – the rape of Pamphile – which
remains insoluble until the intervention of Habrotonon and the revelation
she brings. Instead, it points to a defence of Pamphile designed to mirror
her own earlier display of loyalty and to manifest, even if in hypothetical
terms, the effect of Charisios' growing self-knowledge.

932ff. Onesimos: With responsibility for the dénouement firmly in
the hands of Habrotonon, why does Menander involve Onesimos in the
process of freeing Charisios from his misapprehension? The highly fragmentary state of the text between 936 ('...this minute come out') and 950
prevents any certain restoration of his role or even the attribution of
speaking parts (see Arnott[4] for one possible scenario). We are forced to
rely therefore largely upon the potential dramatic effect of his inclusion,
which suggests (1) since he was instrumental in recovering the ring, he
here provides an element of balance at the point of solution; (2) it allows
a final comic variation on the theme of his master's hostility towards him,
a visual representation of what was described at the beginning of Act III
and at 902ff.; (3) if Arnott's restoration and attribution of 936ff. are

correct (*'Onesimos:* ...come out. How can I keep it from you? – I've achieved such things for you, by Zeus...'), it may mark an attempt to reverse the earlier break-up of the marriage by further revelation. This time, though, there is no effect since Charisios will not listen to him; and (4) it prepares for Onesimos' role in Act V.

951. The woman tempted me: An echo of Onesimos' resolve at the end of Act III to keep out of trouble, but which here serves to shift the emphasis to Habrotonon.

954. I wish it did: For the slowness of a character to accept deliverance from an unbearable situation compare Terence's *The Mother-in-Law* 841ff.

Act V

Once again with the conversion of ignorance and misapprehension into knowledge and understanding the end of Act IV has seen resolution of the problem at the heart of the play. From this, in turn, stems the reconciliation of the young couple, which we may presume took place in the choral interlude preceding Act V. Certainly, its inevitability required no elaboration by representation on stage; its basis was already well established by the young wife's defence of her husband and Charisios' reaction to it, both of which provide ample evidence that the only circumstance keeping them apart was the erroneous interpretation of the rape (cf. *The Girl from Samos*). Act V therefore exists to portray the effects of the plot's resolution, from which the other purpose of final Acts in New Comedy, i.e., tying up loose ends, flows with natural ease. In *The Arbitration* this consists of rewarding those that have helped the young couple – Chairestratos and Habrotonon – and humiliating Smikrines who, while not actually personifying the major obstacle to the plot, as Knemon does in *Old Cantankerous*, does share with him the role of the play's principal ogre. Significantly too, as Sandbach[1] p. 369f. points out, just as the predicament of Charisios and Pamphile was earlier acted out largely through surrogates, so the results of their reconciliation are likewise represented by those around them.

982. Chairestratos: The identity of the character who opens Act V is not given anywhere in the papyrus and has been the cause of considerable dispute, especially since the mention of Chairestratos by name suggests *prima facie* involvement of at least one other character. Suggestions in the past for the identity of this second figure have included Simias, whose name appears fleetingly in a fragmentary address by Karion at 630, and

Onesimos. Neither, however, produces a convincing scenario and it is more likely that the insertion of the name forms part of a self-address (similar to that by Sostratos at *Old Cantankerous* 214ff.) in which Chairestratos reveals his love for Habrotonon, but as a result of loyalty to his friend despairs of being able to win her.

987. she's no slave: A pointer to Habrotonon's character rather than her social status, which remains that of a slave. Whether she does in fact receive her freedom in Act V we cannot tell from the extant text, though its desirability referred to at 539, and the strong undercurrent of natural justice in New Comedy, together with Chairestratos' evident attachment to her, suggest this as a probable development.

1060f. He...off her: Once again the dramatic action in the lacuna before the lines, like the exact significance of the lines themselves, must remain speculative. At best, following Arnott[4], they form part of a monologue from Charisios, who by now has convinced his friend that there is no emotional tie between himself and Habrotonon, and has sent Chairestratos off to declare his love for her. Following this, he observes wistfully that, had their roles been reversed, Chairestratos would not have been as restrained as he himself was, an observation that is not without its own irony since Charisios' earlier behaviour was caused not by loyalty to a friend but by his love for Pamphile.

1062. Sophrone: Why has Menander chosen to introduce the figure of Sophrone when available evidence suggests she has no speaking part and the role Smikrines envisages for her in this further attempt to end his daughter's marriage is hardly essential? Does she exist in fact to provide further, comic, illustration of the old man's wrong-headed plans – now totally otiose – through her reluctance to fall in with them, and then to highlight through the speed with which she grasps the truth the slowness of Smikrines' own mental processes?

1065. *my* dowry-money: Once again the motivation for Smikrines' actions centres upon finance.

1075. The door's locked: This was an unusual event during the day, as Theopropides shows in Plautus' *The Ghost* 444, but is necessary to allow the coming scene with Onesimos to be portrayed in the open.

1079ff. old Grumpy...: Onesimos' immediate reaction to Smikrines sets the comic atmosphere for the exchange, which emphasises the gulf between the knowledge of the one and the continuing misapprehension of the other. In many respects the scene is reminiscent of those which close *Old Cantankerous* (931ff., 960ff.) in the lecture read to the old man and the warning at 1110f. Similarly the complaint about his carelessness in looking after his daughter at 1115 finds an echo in that directed at Knemon by Daos at *Old Cantankerous* 220ff.

1084ff. Do you really think...: Onesimos' sermon is a patchwork of political and philosophic ideas, some vaguely Epicurean, others Stoic, designed not to present any consistent theme – what he says contains too many palpable distortions for that – but to raise a wry smile at the incongruity of a slave dabbling in the subject with the resultant travesty of logic (cf. Arnott[4] p. 512 n.1).

1093f. He's put a guardian in each one of us: A variation on the idea that each human being has a *daimon* or guiding spirit, which some philosophers identified with one's character, cf. Menander fr. 714 'Each man has a *daimon* at his side from the moment of his birth, a beneficent guide throughout life'. The sentiment also finds echoes in the words of Gorgias at *Old Cantankerous* 274ff. and n.

1116. five-month babies: Onesimos aptly avoids a more blatant reference to pre-marital sex, since such a gestation period would not produce a viable infant.

1117. I don't know what you're talking about: Smikrines' continuing obtuseness, despite the mention of 'grandson' in 1112, forms the major source of comedy in these closing sections. Menander in fact ensures its development by placing in Onesimos' mouth allusions to the truth that are clear enough to the audience but sufficiently oblique to prevent automatic comprehension by those on stage. This then allows the development of the contrast between the reactions of Sophrone and Smikrines, a contrast subsequently underlined by the old man's failure to see immediately the relevance of the quotation from Euripides' *Auge*, itself ironic in view of the flattering description from Syros at 325f.

The Rape of the Locks

Act I

Though the play shares with *The Arbitration* a greater fragmentation of text than was the case with *Old Cantankerous* and *The Girl from Samos*, the extent and positioning of the gaps produces a significant increase in problems for detailed interpretation. So for instance, though it is certain the action opened with at least one scene before the divine prologue, little unanimity exists as to the events depicted. Reference to Glykera at 127 confirms that she has already been seen on stage, and this is probably also true of Polemon in view of 129 (lit. 'the explosive man *here*', though the inherent ambiguity of such phrasing and parallels elsewhere in the context of characters who have specifically not been seen precludes absolute certainty). Similarly, the lack of any preparation for the entry of Sosias at 172, when compared to the explicit reference to Doris at 182, strongly suggests that he too has already appeared before the audience. That it is also Sosias who is referred to as witnessing the encounter between the young couple at 154ff. is suggested by the failure to intervene (something the impetuous Polemon would hardly have omitted), just as Daos fails to intervene at *Old Cantankerous* 212ff. What is less likely, however, is that the encounter between Moschion and Glykera was portrayed on stage. At 153, for instance, it is described as having occurred 'yesterday evening', and while action spread over two days is not without parallel in New Comedy (cf. Terence's *The Self-Tormentor* 410, Sandbach[1] p. 326), its rarity counsels caution before we introduce it here. The play may have opened, therefore, with the entry of Polemon and Sosias, who recounted the events of the previous evening. Following this may have come a meeting between the soldier and his mistress in which the contrast between the loving welcome of the one and the mounting rage of the other was developed, culminating in the 'rape of the locks', either on stage, if 167f. is to have its full effect, or off stage, and followed by Polemon's departure to drown his sorrows like Charisios' in *The Arbitration*.

An alternative, no less convincing, scenario, however, is presented by Arnott[9] using the evidence of wall painting in Ephesus. This ostensibly shows a scene from the play involving three characters, who may be interpreted as Glykera, Polemon and Sosias. Arguing that the tableau depicted comes from the lost opening, Arnott suggests that the play began with the entry of Glykera, already shorn, followed by Polemon, by now regretting his hasty action and rebuffed by his mistress, while Sosias looks on (see further Zagagi[2] p. 72f.).

128. the explosive man: An important pointer to the delineation of Polemon's behaviour throughout the play. As Fortenbaugh p. 435 states, it explains not merely the unpremeditated act of cutting off Glykera's hair, but also his constant tendency towards precipitate and vehement action. This manifests itself, for instance, in his reaction to Pataikos at 486ff., which ranges from heated protestations to gloomy despair, and his insistence on the old man seeing Glykera's wardrobe. It subsequently resurfaces in his excessive response to Doris at 982f., his determination to celebrate Glykera's discovery of her father without the proper preliminaries (997ff.), his impulsive departure rather than face Pataikos, suggested for stage action at 1003ff. (fragmentary in the Greek text), and ironically in the very force of his promise to give up vehement action at 1018ff. (see further 164 n.).

129. a native-born Corinthian: We cannot tell why Menander chose to set his play in Corinth rather than the more usual Athens, but the location is guaranteed both by the emphasis upon Corinth here and at 125, and by the fact that Polemon has bought a house which serves as part of the backcloth to the action, something he could not have done as a Corinthian in Athens. In other respects the playwright maintains the underlying premises of Athenian citizenship law, which explains why Glykera's foundling status prevents her from being anything but the soldier's mistress until her recognition by Pataikos (see further Sandbach[1] p. 470, Harrison p. 25ff.).

135. gave her the baby-clothes: Insertion of the reference to these at this early stage suggests that like the ring in *The Arbitration* or similar birth tokens in Euripidean plays (*Ion* 1351ff.) they will form the means by which objective recognition of Glykera's true identity will later be established.

138. if ever she needed help: As a woman Glykera was deemed to be legally incompetent, and hence could only seek redress for injury through her guardian, Moschion. That the two are by now in vastly different social and economic circumstances, however, provides the reason (detailed at 148ff.) why she has not already revealed her relationship to her brother, which in turn forms the foundation for the play's complications. Glykera's superior understanding of the situation likewise provides a moral explanation for her reaction to Moschion's kiss, precluding as it does the forbidden relationship mentioned at 141.

141. I'm IGNORANCE: Like Chance in *The Shield*, the choice of Misapprehension as the speaker of the prologue represents a highly relevant pointer to the main line of plot development, since it is their ignorance of the truth that causes both Moschion and Polemon to act as they do, from which in turn derives the widespread dramatic irony of the play.

144. *not* reliable: The description probably refers not so much to Polemon's character as to the fact that his profession might take him away from Glykera at any moment, hence the need to keep Moschion as a hypothetical source of help in an emergency.

147. she's living next door to her brother: Comic coincidence, upon which many of the events of New Comedy are based.

149. his apparent social standing: The use of 'apparent' here cannot be fortuitous. Since legal adoption excluded foundlings (Harrison p. 87), it suggests that Moschion is being passed off as the legitimate offspring of Myrrina and her husband, a status that would be spoilt if Glykera made her relationship to him public. That she does not do so, even after her treatment at Polemon's hands, is not only necessary on a technical level – to allow continuation of the plot – but also serves to manifest the considerable regard she has for her brother's best interests.

159. he marched off: i.e., Moschion.

164f. He's not really like that: An instance of Menander's ability to transform the stock characteristics of the soldier type (e.g., Pyrgopolynices in Plautus' *The Swaggering Soldier*) into something more sophisticated (Goldberg[2] p. 46f. compares Thrasonides in *The Man She Hated*, cf. MacCary[3] p. 285). As Arnott[4] p. xxxiiif. points out, while Polemon displays almost all the characteristics of the stock type, they are constantly revised into something new and unexpected: he is hot tempered and driven by jealousy into precipitate and harsh action, but as 172ff. indicates, he undergoes an almost immediate collapse of emotional force into someone more deserving of the audience's sympathy than its opprobrium. Though he lacks the extreme stupidity of the Plautine model, he nevertheless has to be shown by Pataikos that his claims upon Glykera's loyalty are ill-founded. Though he is no coward, he relies on others to re-establish contact with his mistress at 504ff. and displays great apprehension at the prospect of facing her newly discovered father at 1003. Though he is not cursed with self-conceit, he takes considerable pride in the clothes he has provided for Glykera.

In this way, since the ultimate goal of the plot is the discovery of Glykera's true identity, from which in turn flows her marriage to Polemon, Menander ensures the credibility of such reconciliation by emphasising that recent violence is not typical of Polemon's behaviour but an extreme and somewhat aberrant manifestation of his temperament. Rather than forego completely the comic potential in the characteristics of the soldier-type, however, Menander skilfully transfers them to others in the play, in particular to Moschion with his self-professed skill as a lady-killer (300ff.), his forwardness (151), his tendency to calculation (152f.) and to leading from the rear (295ff.), but also to Sosias with his martial language at the beginning of Act II and his absurd posturing as a military figure in Act III (Goldberg[2] p. 49f., Fortenbaugh p. 436f., Brenk p. 40f.).

I led him on: Misapprehension does not suggest active intervention on her part to cause Polemon's behaviour, but rather that she created a situation specifically designed to provoke a response that would lead to the recognition of father and daughter (cf. Zagagi[2] p.73f.).

168. thought it 'disgusting': The Greek text makes no mention of the 'scene', so that Misapprehensions's reference here may not be to anything specific, such as the actual cutting of Glykera's hair as many have supposed, but rather to the whole situation.

170f. Goodbye...coming: The *captatio benevolentiae* as at *Old Cantankerous* 45f.

Ladies and Gentlemen: lit. 'onlookers', cf. *Old Cantankerous* 194 n.

174. he's in floods of tears: The description acts as an antidote to any hostility the audience may feel towards Polemon's earlier harsh treatment of Glykera. His contrition, the result of recognising he has acted wrongly and unjustly (cf. Fortenbaugh p. 432), is reminiscent indeed of Charisios' reaction to his wife's defence in *The Arbitration*.

177ff. He's...cloak: cf. Parmenon's errand in *The Girl from Samos* Act V. Despite the slave's parting remark ('he just wants to keep me on the trot'), inserted for its comic value, the errand is patently designed as a reconnaissance mission, to discover the situation inside Polemon's house, and is later repeated at 354f. where Sosias re-enters bringing with him the soldier's cloak and sword. The mention of the sword there and use of the word *chlamys* (lit. military cloak), in contrast to the more general term *himation* used here, suggests that the garment Polemon wants is not an army cloak, as the translation implies, but a civilian one. On his first entry, fresh from military service, Polemon would have been in uniform. The need to change into civilian dress now forms the pretext for Sosias' mission, just as later, once changed, he sends the slave back home carrying his military gear.

181. I'll go and see, madam: Use of the address 'madam' (lit. 'mistress') immediately identifies Doris as a slave. Her errand is presumably to discover if Myrrhine will allow Glykera to take refuge in her house next door, while her next statement, preparing to knock, is reminiscent of Getas' more broadly humorous grumbles at *Old Cantankerous* 456ff.

188ff. He'll be pleased...wanted: Editors are divided over whether these lines should be given to Doris or, with somewhat greater appropriateness, to Sosias, whose prediction of Polemon's pleasure at learning of Glykera's tears is ironic in view of 172ff.

261. a crowd of young lads: On the conventional announcement of the chorus' first entry see *Old Cantankerous* 230f. n. Like Daos' misinterpretation of the dialogue between Sostratos and Knemon's daughter in the earlier play, the slave's ignorance of recent events leads to radical distortion in the report he will deliver to Moschion, with a consequent increase in overall misapprehension.

Act II

Once again Menander minimises the impact of the choral interlude by providing (1) an effective bridge between Acts in the person of Daos; (2) the illusion that we come upon master and slave in mid-conversation; and (3) continuity of theme through depicting the results that stem from Daos' intentions at the end of Act I (cf. *Old Cantankerous* Acts I-II). As far as 353 the action is set in longer lines (trochaic tetrameter), often used in scenes of increased liveliness such as *The Girl from Samos* 421-615, 670ff. but also found where a more serious tone is required, as at *Old Cantankerous* 708-83. The present instance, with its strong element of unreality and frustrated expectations, clearly belongs to the former category.

272ff. *I* managed the whole thing...: Why has Menander made Daos the author of such patently false claims when their falsehood becomes clear within the space of fifty lines? Are they designed, like the shift in metre and the banter over rewards, to bring into sharp focus the unreality of the situation, allowing it to intensify as Moschion swallows the slave's account (despite his qualms at 267f.) before its devastating collison with reality?

283. I'd rather keep a general store: This was the trade of many ex-slaves, and fleeting hopes of freedom may underpin Daos' suggestion. Clearly, though, the main dramatic effect of the statement comes from the comic bathos of his ambition after the inflated promises from Moschion.

295ff. You go in first: The instruction is a powerful indicator that for all his boldness in stealing a kiss from Glykera, the young man is essentially a braggart who depends heavily upon the actions of others. The scene now mirrors, in the contrast of intention and result, Moschion's ruse in *The Girl from Samos* 657ff., with the slave's absence providing the opportunity for a demonstration of his master's optimistic reverie and the scheming side to his character as he plans how best to flatter his mother.

301. she didn't run away: Menander relies upon the audience's superior knowledge to underline the irony in Moschion's interpretation of his sister's behaviour.

304. if I may say so without offence: lit. a reference to Adrasteia, at times identified with Nemesis, inserted by Moschion to avert divine displeasure at his boastfulness, but which merely highlights his self-conceit (cf. Sostratos' reference to Pan at *Old Cantankerous* 571ff.).

305. She's bathed, and sitting there: By his description of Glykera in terms typical of the *hetaira* awaiting her lover, Daos raises further both Moschion's expectations of an easy conquest and the audience's anticipation of comic disaster.

325. you've done me down!: Like Sostratos in his reaction to Pyrrhias at *Old Cantankerous* 138ff., Moschion vents his annoyed disappointment upon the slave – in this play, though, with greater justice. The playwright has arranged, in fact, the depiction not of a single disappointment but of two, since Daos is as much perplexed by the collapse of his earlier interpretation as is his master. This duality of comic interplay continues indeed as Daos attempts to backtrack on his earlier assertions, establishing a new scenario, one more in keeping with present evidence and no less favourable to his master (and hence to himself) but, as the audience knows, no less bogus.

341. Now you're talking: The words indicate Moschion's continuing naïvety: his readiness to accept the latest twist in Daos' story when the first proved so patently false, when the account of what has just occurred indoors ostensibly rules out the possibility of Daos' having acquired any objective understanding of Glykera's attitude, and when this latest version is introduced by a highly significant 'Perhaps' (337). The essential unreality of Daos' claims is further increased by introducing what 318ff. seems to have precluded – the intervention of Glykera herself: 'She told me so' (343).

343. for three or four days: This is all part of the new reality in Daos' attempt to establish Glykera as no common call-girl (lit. music girl) or street-walker (as contemptuous a term in Greek as it is in English) who might serve for a one-night stand, but someone who intends a more long-lasting affair with Moschion, already signalled by the departure from her previous lover. From the audience's viewpoint such a scenario is even more ludicrous than the one which opened the Act.

348. You don't...*think*: Menander probably intended the protestation to carry a double significance. In terms of stage dialogue it attempts to rebut Moschion's charge of unintelligibility with the claim that the young man's impatience has not allowed Daos to formulate his thoughts properly. In reality, however, that impatience is as much an obstacle to the slave's production of a consistent, if spurious, tale as Theopropides' questions are to Tranio in Plautus' *The Ghost* 659ff.; hence the observation 'That was close' in 352.

359f. I've never seen Master so miserable: Following the longer lines of the previous scene, which compounded the unreality of Daos' fabrications, the exchange between the two slaves returns to the slower metre of normal dialogue (iambic trimeter). Before the banter which characterises their meeting, however, Menander is careful to remind his audience of Polemon's true emotional state in contrast to the glib bellicosity to come. Nevertheless, in a play based upon rival claims to the attention of a woman – for all that such claims are misplaced on one side – Menander clearly could not neglect the opportunity to produce a scene of conflict, but chose to represent it not between the principal characters involved but between surrogate slaves, thereby increasing the potential for comedy and avoiding a clash between figures soon to be connected by marriage.

364. *our* Master: Though the absence of Myrrhine's husband both facilitates Glykera's move next door and renders the threatened attack on the house (388f.) more of a possibility, the reference may have been designed primarily to foreshadow his later involvement in the action. Damage to the text, however, prevents certainty in this.

372. I'll go and knock: The real function of Daos' failure to follow his master indoors is to prevent Sosias from approaching Myrrhine's house. In this way the audience is treated to a comical clash of wills motivated by Sosias' need to know if Glykera really is next door.

376. her legal guardian: A fiction, as 497 makes clear, but the claim is designed to impute an illegal act to Moschion and his helper by representing Glykera's self-motivated absence as a kind of kidnapping.

380f. pound-an-hour...tuppeny-ha'penny: lit. 'four obols ($^2/3$ drachma)...four drachmas'. Despite variation of textual restoration and interpretation, Daos' jibe is clearly aimed at suggesting Polemon and his household are anything but crack troops and will easily be overcome in any struggle.

384. Hilarion!: Why is the name introduced only to make the character unavailable as a witness? Damage to the Greek text at this point produces a wide spectrum of possible scenarios. Does the departure of Hilarion serve, for example, to underline the very incongruity of Sosias' threats, made as they are from a position of weakness that characterises his role in the whole exchange? Does it indicate the frustration of his efforts at every stage, both by Daos and by the actions of those who should be on his side?

389. this 'bijou residence': lit. 'this wretched little house' deliberately disparaging what, from Misapprehension's description of Moschion's current status in society, was doubtless an opulent establishment.

390. the Great Lover: lit. 'the adulterer', designed to insult, like its earlier use at 370 ('her boyfriend'), and to amuse by the grotesqueness of its implications. Like Polemon at 489 Sosias overstates his case, here though for the comic potential of his bluster.

397. Doris: Stage activity remains a source of difficulty. Where, for instance, does Doris emerge from and why? The translation presupposes she comes from Myrrhine's house, though this would mean she would have to pass Daos on the very threshold without any reference to the fact. As Bain[1] p. 121 n.4 argues (cf. Frost p. 94), it is perhaps more likely that she emerges from the house of Polemon, whose property she still is. Indeed she may have followed Sosias on stage at 366f., one of the servants he there abused and now continues to abuse, this time though as a result of his frustrated anger at Daos. As a witness to the dispute between the other two she naturally attempts to intervene after Daos' exit in order to put the record straight (especially in view of Daos' flat denial that Glykera is in Myrrhine's house). This she does by confirming what at 369f. was only supposition on Sosias' part, and assuring him that the reason for the move was not to be near Moschion but to escape Polemon's violence.

Act III

Damage to the text at the beginning of Act III precludes any certainty in reconstructing the scenario involved, beyond establishing Pataikos in the role of honest broker, since he is apparently on friendly terms with both Polemon and Myrrhine. Considerations, therefore, of whether he accompanied Polemon on stage, entered separately from a different direction, or emerged from his own house must remain in the realm of speculation (see further Sandbach[1] p. 501f., Frost p. 95). Certainly the suggestion that Pataikos is in some way related to Myrrhine or even her husband would seem to be precluded by the absolute silence of the Prologue on the matter.

467f. He's been bribed...traitor...: This is clearly the over-reaction of a drunken slave attempting to prevent any meaningful dialogue between the other two when it threatens his plans to storm Myrrhine's house. Menander's insertion of the theme serves in fact to lighten the beginning of an otherwise earnest exchange.

471f. I had no more than one glass: The protestation seems designed either for the sake of comedy pure and simple or, more likely, to renew audience sympathy for Polemon by showing he has not taken the obvious escape route from self-reproach and self-pity.

484. frontal assault...*can't* you?: From Habrotonon's reaction, the phrasing of the question involves a degree of sexual *double entendre*, further intensified by application of the vulgar and insulting term 'tart' (485) and indicative of Sosias' pique at not being allowed to carry through his plans. The jibes are inserted, however, not merely as gratuitous slurs but to clear the stage of extraneous characters so that attention can be concentrated upon Polemon and Pataikos. The hypothesis of Sosias' continued presence on stage, sunk into a drunken stupor, is based solely on Moschion's later reference 'Sosias here' at 531. That this need not imply actual presence any more than it does in the case of Smikrines at *The Shield* 139, lays open the possibility in fact that Sosias leaves with the rest (Frost p. 96 n.17). Certainly, to retain the slave on stage would require an unparalleled fourth speaking part to play Moschion when he enters at 526 and would thus breach the generally accepted premise that New Comedy was written for performance by no more than three speaking actors (see further *The Sikyonian* 272ff. n.).

487. lawful wedded wife: The reference forms one of the main points of misapprehension upon which the play is founded: Polemon's belief that his relationship to Glykera allowed him to demand from a mistress the loyalty and faithfulness that were the hallmarks of a wife. In itself, such a belief is not an altogether negative factor, since it implies the genuineness and strength of his feelings for Glykera. The purpose of Pataikos' subsequent question 'Who 'gave away the bride'?', however, is to demonstrate Glykera's non-citizen status and in consequence her inability to contract a legal marriage, which in Athenian law (and Corinthian law too, for the purposes of this play) required both parties to be of full citizen status (cf. 129 n.). It follows, therefore, that in the absence of any legal tie all that bound the two together was mutual emotional attachment, which Polemon's brutal action has effectively severed. Furthermore, any attempted violent resumption of his control over Glykera by storming Myrrhine's house makes him liable in turn to the due processes of law (see further Brenk p. 42f.).

493. Not *treating* her properly?: The question is ironic for an audience that fully appreciates the dichotomy between the viewpoints of Glykera and Polemon, who for all his contrition, continues to regard himself as the first to have suffered injury as a result of the stolen kiss.

499. the man who seduced her: A further aspect of Polemon's misapprehension in that he has no evidence of any sexual contact between Glykera and Moschion, but merely extrapolates from circumstantial evidence and his hot-headed imagination.

500. you can charge him with it: The reference is deliberately vague since there is no indication of any legal redress for enticing away someone in Glykera's position. The most that Polemon can perhaps do is lodge a private complaint with Moschion.

504f. I don't know what to say: The outburst completely shifts the direction of the dialogue. So far it has been Pataikos who has taken the lead, steering the soldier towards a proper understanding of his position. From now on it is Polemon who dominates the exchange, persuading Pataikos to intervene on his behalf, but in a way calculated to emphasise his desperation by (1) the chiasmic repetition of the fact Glykera has left him (506f. cf. *The Girl from Samos* 535-41, where the repetition is similarly a mark of deep emotion); (2) the lack of proper structure in his sentences at 507-10 and 514-16; (3) his obsession, first with persuading Pataikos to intervene on his behalf – despite the fact that the old man's immediate agreement to do so (510) makes further appeals otiose – and then with irrelevancies such as Glykera's wardrobe and height, as he himself recognises at 522f. ('That's nothing to do with the case') and (4) the frantic repetition of appeals to Pataikos' name at 507, 512 (where a second instance occurs in the Greek linked to 'you must'), at 517, and probably too after 'wardrobe' in the textually disputed line 524.

515. just come...for her – : Menander inserts a perceptive insight into the psychology of the male tendency to display affection through gifts (cf. Demeas in *The Girl from Samos* 377ff., Fantham p. 50, Arnott[3] p. 151f.) which suddenly replaces Polemon's no less vehement protestations of devotion (cf. 128 n.).

526. Moschion: The text does not indicate anywhere at what point Moschion, who must have been eavesdropping on the other two for some time, becomes visible to the audience. His entrance may indeed be as sudden and unexpected as that of Gorgias at *Old Cantankerous* 821, or the mention of Sosias at 531 may imply that Moschion had entered at some point after 485 (when the rest of Polemon's army left the stage) and had been lurking in the background. As Frost p. 96 notes, the young man's bravado has an element of irony about it, since he has evidently waited for Polemon to disappear before hurling insults at him. This is, however, as essential a requirement in a situation where the two will eventually become brothers-in-law, as was the similar prevention of any significant contact between Knemon and Sostratos in *Old Cantankerous*.

535f. as miserable as me: What is the cause of Moschion's wretchedness? The evidence of the extant text suggests a further manifestation of the young man's unrequited love for Glykera, ironic in the eyes of an audience aware that he and Polemon are as united in this as they are separated by the antagonism of their rival claims. In a wider context, however, the loss of text after 550 may mask the possibility that his wretchedness is caused by the discovery of evidence suggesting a blood tie between himself and Glykera. Certainly by 774, when he next appears, Moschion has reason to believe Glykera may be his sister, but whether he was made aware of this before his entry at 526, or in a dialogue with his mother in the lost section after 550, is impossible to tell (Sandbach[1] p. 511ff.).

537f. I did none of the things I normally do: A further instance of the calculation that marked Moschion's monologue at 311ff. and, as the final extant words in 550 suggest ('I was rehearsing a speech'), probably no less doomed to take a different path from the one intended.

Act IV

As is the case with other plays, Act IV brings with it what seems to be the crisis of the action, and also its resolution. In the present instance, however, the crisis which develops is brought about not by any outside interference, such as Smikrines introduces in *The Arbitration*, but by Glykera's own reaction to events. This provides in fact a mirror image to Polemon's role in Act III, but also threatens to render permanent the rift between them as a result of the forthright spirit of self-respect she displays. In true Menandrean fashion, however, it is the very strength of Glykera's feelings here, the obstacle she creates to any further contact with Polemon, that ultimately brings about what for the moment seems impossible.

710f. he wouldn't marry a girl like me: lit. 'He's in quite the same social class as me'. Glykera's pointed observation firmly rejects the first of two possible, if unsavoury, interpretations of her taking refuge with Myrrhine – a desire to marry Moschion. The absurdity of such a union between a rich freeborn male and a foundling who is also a soldier's cast-off was self-evident and needed no further expansion. Its insertion indeed serves merely as introduction to the second, more serious scenario. To the audience, on the other hand, her words contain multiple levels of irony, aware as they are:

1) that Glykera knows marriage is ruled out by ties of blood far more effectively than by class;

2) that Moschion's social standing, which Glykera continues to protect for all her present plight, needs ultimately no protection;

3) that she directs her arguments to a man who is her long-lost father – if there was some indication of this in a now-lost section of the prologue.

711ff. To become his mistress?: The force of Glykera's argument here is backed up by the balanced phrasing she introduces: '*I*'d have been anxious...and so would *he...he*'s established...and *I*'ve apparently...'.

713. he's established me in his father's house: Glykera's rejection of the second possibility (ironic in so far as this was precisely Moschion's intention) stems from a demonstration of the illogicality that underlies it – the fact that (1) the affair envisaged would have suggested secrecy and caution, not its open flaunting in the young man's home, and (2) had Glykera's move next door been motivated by a desire to become Moschion's mistress, she would inevitably have earned Myrrhine's hostility. This has not materialised, therefore the move was not caused by any attachment to Moschion.

723f. find some other girl to insult: Glykera's reference in the Greek to *hybris* (cf. *Old Cantankerous* 298 n.) underpins her sense of grievance: her belief that for all Polemon's ignorance of the relationship between herself and Moschion that led to misinterpretation of the kiss, his reaction went far beyond all that was morally right. Ironically, through the depth of his remorse Polemon has come to regard his act in much the same way; hence the embarrassment at facing his mistress and his use of an intermediary instead.

745f. Just do as I ask: Does the fact that Glykera fails to answer Pataikos' previous question introduce subtle foreshadowing of ultimate reconciliation? Does it suggest perhaps that the stand she takes, laudable in a character the audience knows is of citizen status and who expects to be treated as such, is not whole-hearted and that for all the hurt she has experienced she still has some feelings for Polemon? Such a conclusion would seem to be necessary if the aim of the plot is a resumption of relations, but this time through marriage.

748f. You ought to think of all that's involved: Pataikos probably refers to the insecurity that will inevitably follow a total break with Polemon (cf. Demeas' picture of Chrysis' future in *The Girl from Samos* 390ff.). The fact that Glykera persists with her course of action despite Pataikos' continuing offers of conciliation again reveals her essential nobility.

755. This is terrible!: What is the cause of Doris' upset? Some have suggested that while Pataikos was being shown Glykera's wardrobe, he recognised and removed items that turn out to be her birth tokens (cf. 135 n.), a loss Doris has subsequently discovered and here laments. The total lack of evidence for this in the extant text, however, needs no demonstration. Furthermore, as Bain[1] p. 122f. observes:

1) Pataikos' behaviour at the beginning of the Act hardly suggests any suspicion that Glykera may be his daughter.

2) Doris' emotional state exists before any mention of the tokens. If it

had been caused by their loss, we might have expected some statement to this effect.

3) Pataikos' interest in the tokens only materialises at 758ff. and is hardly the reaction of a man to the mention of something he already has in his possession.

On available evidence, therefore, Doris' upset is best taken as simply her reaction to the break-down of relations between Glykera and Polemon, just as Demeas' household is thrown into disorder by the ejection of Chrysis at *The Girl from Samos* 440ff.

756. the little box: Though damage to the papyrus has removed all trace of the word, its restoration is supported by analogies elsewhere in New Comedy: Terence's *The Eunuch* 753, Plautus' *Cistellaria* 655ff. and *The Rope* 1078, 1133.

758f. Now that's queer: Textual problems make stage action at this point problematical. Is Pataikos' statement a response to the sight of the box or something inside it as the translation suggests, or is it caused by some recollection of having already seen the box in question? And is this recollection, like that at 768 'I've seen a piece of embroidery like that before' (lit. '[*lacuna*] I saw then also') a reference to years ago or when Polemon recently showed him Glykera's wardrobe?

774ff. It's not impossible...: Again stage action is open to varied interpretation, making this either an aside commenting on the dialogue of the other two, or more likely an entrance monologue in view of the utterance's length, the style in which it is set, and the difficulty that would be created for maintaining the three-actor rule if Moschion entered any earlier (see further 484 n., Bain[1] p. 113ff.).

779: At this point the recognition scene begins. It is written in a style reminiscent of Greek Tragedy in the exhaustive examination of evidence before recognition is acknowledged (cf. 824 n.), in the formal alternation of whole lines between speakers (*stichomythia*) as far as 810, and in the application of stricter verse patterns more usually associated with tragedy. The *stichomythia* element extends even to the deliberate insertion of redundant material, either to maintain the alternation of lines (780 'Go on...you like') or to ensure the completion of whole lines (in contrast to the effect in 723-60 and 810ff. where exchanges begin and end within lines), e.g. 'Tell me' (785), 'May I know?' (799), 'you frighten me' (805), 'Heavens, how dreadful!' (807). The tragic flavour is further strengthened by ostensibly deliberate echoes of Euripidean phrasing at 788 ('Then how did you come to be separated?'), which is reminiscent of Euripides fr. 484 from the otherwise lost *Melanippe the Wise* 'When they were separated from one another', and at 809 ('had foundered...sea'), which echoes *The Women from Troy* 88 'I shall shake the surge of the Aegean sea' (cf. Goldberg[2] p. 54). Does the introduction of such tragic elements, however, signify Menander's wish to enhance the seriousness of the scene or does it betoken parody, as some have suggested? Or does the presence throughout the exchange of a character like Moschion, who has consistently been portrayed in a comic light, itself prevent the scene from taking on too pronounced an air of seriousness without recourse to parody? A final answer to such questions is clearly impossible; the contrasting overtones introduced by the playwright evoke so wide a range of possible response as to preclude any hope of certainty. The most we might perhaps say is that in the search for novelty in an already well-worn device, Menander points to the incongruity of a tragic form, usually associated with heroic figures, in the context of family life and a fractured love affair (see further Sandbach[1] p. 519f., Turner[1] p. 126ff., Bain[1] p. 115ff.).

787. That answers one of my questions: In addition to possible lightening of the atmosphere, Moschion's asides also inject an element of economy into the drama, ensuring that while the scene concentrates upon the more significant character of Glykera, recognition of identity is actually achieved for both. In this way, Menander avoids a dissipation of dramatic force that would result from repetition of the recognition process with someone who is never fully developed but remains essentially a comic counterpart to Polemon.

789ff. I *could* tell: Even now Glykera continues to protect her brother's present good fortune (cf. 147ff.).

792. Another piece of clear confirmation!: A reference perhaps to factors mentioned in the gap after 550: Myrrhine had told Moschion that the identity of his sister was known, but had refused any further clarification.

799. Who was that?: So far it has been Pataikos who has controlled the exchange by his questioning; now Glykera takes over that role as far as 810, allowing the injection of additional pathos as she elicits from her father the story of her own exposure as a child. Significantly, in this section of deepening emotion, there is no interruption from Moschion to inject an element of comedy.

817. I haven't got it any longer: Despite extensive damage to the text at this point ('my brother has it' is a conjectural supplement in the translation), restoration of the dialogue's sense nevertheless remains possible. Mention of a brooch no longer in her possession followed by Moschion's realisation that Pataikos must be his father suggests that by now Moschion either has the brooch himself or has at least been shown it by Myrrhine. From this comes the final clue to confirm his link with Glykera.

824. My darling daughter!: Only now does Menander provide a statement of formal recognition, despite the fact that its presumption has formed the basis of the exchange since 772f. (cf. 800). In this way the playwright is able to develop the pathos of the situation to the full.

827. Heavens, who's this?: We cannot be sure who speaks the question – whether Pataikos or Glykera – but it signifies surprise rather than simple ignorance of Moschion's identity, a reaction to the interrupted embrace of father and daughter.

Act V

As Misapprehension makes clear at 165ff., the main aim of the play is the reunion of parent and children, an event which finds its fulfilment in Act IV, leaving Act V once again to clear up loose ends, in particular, the relationship between Glykera and Polemon. A further feature of final Acts seen so far has been the discomfiture of those who have caused major complications. Though in the present case no obvious ogre-figure exists, two characters have been instrumental in causing problems. The first is Polemon himself, who throughout the action has been paying for his impetuous behaviour with self-inflicted reproaches and despair. From what remains of Act V this would seem to continue and even to intensify before its resolution, as he probably realises that Glykera's new-found status makes his treatment of her all the more unacceptable and any reconciliation even more unlikely. The other character involved in creating problems is Moschion, and the end of the extant text, showing Pataikos planning to marry him to the daughter of Philinos, doubtless signals the need for him to abandon amorous escapades and in future to direct his affections towards more socially acceptable ends (cf. Clitipho in Terence's *The Self-Tormentor*).

979. She'll come back to you – : The reasons for Glykera's willingness to return to Polemon have been variously restored by commentators to fill the gap between Acts IV and V. To what extent these figured within the detailed stage action, however, we shall perhaps never know.

982f. I'll set you free tomorrow: Like Polemon's willingness to do anything, the reward promised to Doris, which is out of keeping with her role as the mere bearer of good news, illustrates both the level of relief he feels on discovering Glykera has not discarded him for ever and his continuing impetuosity (cf. 128 n.).

996. The cook's already in the house: The caterer was conventionally hired for special occasions, though how and when he got into Polemon's house is unexplained in the extant text and may (*pace* Sandbach[1]) need no explanation in these closing sections of the play.

1003. how can I face her father?: If restoration and interpretation of the fragmentary text at this point are correct, stage action is now firmly embedded in the comic atmosphere essential for the happy ending, as Polemon is temporarily removed from the stage by embarrassment in order to allow a brief scene between Glykera and Pataikos confirming the reconciliation from their standpoint. The fact that the two enter in mid-conversation, with Pataikos referring to offstage remarks by Glykera, allows her to be played by a mute from this point on with no loss of dramatic reality. Instead she simply reverts to the normal, silent role for a free-born girl in the power of her father. (Assignment of 1021f., 'This time...all' and 1023, 'So...forgiveness', to Glykera in the papyrus is doubtless wrong, since it would require either a fourth speaking part, some excessively rapid costume changing, or a definite pause in the action to allow this to take place.)

1013f. I formally give her to you in marriage: Pataikos' words provide formal recognition that the reconciliation is now complete and the union of Polemon and Glykera restored, this time though, in view of Glykera's altered status, in the only proper form available – marriage.

1015. a handsome dowry: lit. three talents (18,000 drachmas).

1018. Good God, no!: Like 982f., or his cavalier approach to the sacrifice at 997ff., Polemon's impetuosity continues to the end, revealed with comic irony even in his resolution to renounce it for ever. Now, however, it is directed towards a positive demonstration of his affection, not the negative jealousy of the play's beginning.

1021f. This time...for us all: At what is virtually the end of the play, Menander inserts a reminder of Misapprehension's assurance at 164ff., bringing the action round full circle.

The Shield

Act I

The Shield is the only one of Menander's extant plays which displays in full the implications of the deferred prologue format for exposition, and its advantages for a work founded upon misapprehension:

1) By allowing an initial development of the situation as known to the human participants it establishes an atmosphere of gloom and despondency calculated to arrest attention by its very incongruity in a comedy.

2) It enables the audience to engage in character evaluation before the objective information that comes from the goddess.

3) It increases the audience's own emotional response by imposing on the action an element of suspense until the introduction of Chance's superior knowledge.

Had the divine prologue been introduced at the beginning of the play, virtually the whole burden of exposition would have fallen upon the goddess. As a result there would have been little for the human characters to do when first seen but to pour out their grief, and any information they provided would run the risk of merely repeating what was already known.

1ff. Daos: Though the opening scene is set in dialogue form, Menander is careful to establish at the outset the essentials upon which an exchange can be built through a concentration of factual and atmospheric details. The incongruity of the situation has already been mentioned. It exists as much in the use of a comic slave in circumstances redolent with tragedy as in the arrival of a baggage train which reverses the normal potential for humour in such an event (cf. *Old Cantankerous* 393ff., 430ff.), and is further emphasised by the use of strict metrical rhythms, more characteristic of tragedy than comedy, in the first nine lines. Similarly, the details given occur not as isolated data divorced from the drama, as they would do if the exposition were established by a prologue, but are immediately set within a credible interwoven context. So for instance, Daos' description of Kleostratos' death is viewed not as an event separate from those involved in the scene, but one that goes far beyond the individual to the ruined hopes of marriage for the young man's sister and a comfortable old age for his tutor, a contrast of former aspirations and present reality that was in fact a conventional feature of ritual lament. The atmosphere of gloom too is immediately established through the regret the young man's death causes in others, which serves in turn as the touchstone by which Smikrines' reaction can be measured.

14. I, your tutor: This self-description by Daos is important since it characterises him from the start as educated, explains his attachment to Kleostratos and the regret felt at his apparent death, suggests an element of validity for the characterisation of Smikrines hinted at in the subsequent dialogue, and renders credible Daos' later role as instigator of the plot against him. Evaluation of the skill with which Menander has established his characters in the play, however, varies. Sandbach[1] (p. 62) views them as lacking in depth and originality: Daos is 'without faults', Smikrines 'wholly bad' (cf. Arnott[4] p. 5). MacCary[1] p. 282 on the other hand sees Daos as the playwright's 'most attractive slave', while Lloyd-Jones[2] (p. 193) refers to him as 'the most loyal and intelligent slave known to us from the specimens of the genre, in Greek and Latin, which we possess'. Such discrepancy indicates perhaps the need to see characterisation in the play not as an absolute factor but one tied closely to the plot being developed. In the case of *The Shield* our knowledge suggests this was inherently simple, devoid to a large extent of the dramatic nuances to be found elsewhere, and as a result simplicity of characterisation may actually have been an advantage.

18. Ah, Daos, little did we think – : lit. 'Oh, the unexpected chance'. Use of the word 'chance' becomes in hindsight an ironic reference to the speaker of the prologue, the 'Controller and Director of the whole story' (147f.), and finds verbal echoes in the Greek throughout the action: 'we'd been *lucky*' (25), '*success*' (27), '*Fortunately*' (58), 'with *luck*' (248), 'Have a *good* death' (381), '*Chance*' (411), '*happiness* to *misery*' (lit. 'unhappiness') (418).

How are we to interpret the brevity of Smikrines' opening remarks? To Sandbach[1] it indicates that the two entered together with Smikrines already aware of his nephew's fate, thereby removing the need for a more overtly emotional response (cf. Frost p. 21f., Blundell p. 72). Equally well, however, in the context of a first meeting between the two actually on stage it might constitute an early indication of Smikrines' inhumanity, his lack of concern except where an element of self-interest intervenes.

19. How did he die?: For much of the first scene Smikrines' role is that of a quasi-protatic character (cf. *Old Cantankerous* 50 n.), whose chief dramatic function is to provide a cue for the disclosure of further details, to steer the audience's reaction, as with 'Lovely!' (33), 'How shocking!' (48), and by the simple expedient of interruption to break up into its individual stages what would otherwise have been a lengthy monologue followed by that from Chance with all the attendant potential for tedium.

33. with his pockets full: Serving soldiers in antiquity, whether attached as mercenaries to some dynast (both Antigonus of Syria and Ptolemy of Egypt contested ownership of Lycia in the final decades of the 4th century BC) or engaged in freebooting raids, regarded the right to loot as an essential element in such conditions of service as they had. Smikrines' reaction 'Lovely!', incongruous in the context of the overall despondency coming from Daos, seems designed in fact to blacken the old man's character. As Goldberg[2] (p. 33) observes, his further interruption in disapproval of the soldiers' celebrations and his approbation of Daos' escape from disaster, like the very mention of his name in 20, conjure up images of the selfish and miserly old man of comedy in contrast to Daos' evident tragic-messenger role.

71f. their faces were all bloated: Behind the understandable reluctance of the survivors to leave their stronghold while the enemy was nearby lies the dramatic need to ensure that casualties could not be recognised except by associated finds (i.e., the shield). The same is true of the decision to conduct a hurried mass-cremation, which prevented Daos from making further, more detailed, inspection of the body. In this way the playwright creates the misapprehension upon which the plot is based.

84. sixteen kilograms: lit. '40 minae', the equivalent of 4,000 drachmas. If, as is likely, the gold coins mentioned in 34 and 82 were staters, each worth 20 drachmas, the total value of Kleostratos' bullion would be 16,000 drachmas or nearly 3 talents, more than enough for his sister's dowry (the motive for his military service). It is additionally ironic, therefore, that Kleostratos' supposed death should have occurred when his task was essentially complete.

85. Your inheritance: Like 'they belong to you' (89), Daos' observation draws immediate attention to the real focus of Smikrines' interest, as the old man unconsciously confirms when, following his immediate denial of concern with such matters, he cannot resist exploring the topic further with 'Was all the rest taken?'. Daos' words also provide economical foreshadowing of subsequent developments, since in Attic law it was not Smikrines who automatically succeeded to his nephew's estate but the young man's sister. As the translator explains (p. 125, cf. MacDowell[2] p. 44ff.), her position is complicated by the fact that the inheritance makes her an *epikleros*, whose hand could be claimed in marriage by her father's nearest male relation, as Smikrines later intends to do.

97ff.: Though Menander reveals in the opening scene those salient factors upon which future difficulties are built, there has so far been nothing upon which New Comedy's major effect, dramatic irony, can be founded. To rectify this, and at the same time to reverse the tone of events from tragedy to comic misapprehension, the playwright brings in the goddess Chance. In addition to introducing other members of Kleostratos' family her role is to disclose the one factor upon which the comedy of the plot is based: that Kleostratos is not dead and will soon return. In this respect the deferred prologue of *The Shield* runs parallel to that in *The Rape of the Locks*, where Misapprehension assured her audience that Polemon's behaviour towards Glykera was the forerunner of reuniting parent and offspring. In *The Shield* the audience is presented with similar foreshadowing through the description of Smikrines' designs upon his nephew's estate and the ultimate failure of his scheme.

Structurally the speech has much in common with that from Pan in *Old Cantankerous* in that the significance of details provided by Chance is often reinforced by their location at the important first and last positions in the lines of verse: 'unpleasant' (97), 'goddess' (98), 'shield' (107, 109), 'He fell immediately' (108), 'Kleostratos' – the only human character named in the Greek text of the prologue (110), 'he'll come back safely' (112), 'twister' (116), 'He wants everything' (120).

if something unpleasant: Though it is not till 108f. that the audience learns the circumstances leading to misidentification of the body, the emphasis Chance here places upon the fact that something unpleasant has *not* occurred (since in Greek theology the gods avoided the pollution associated with death) both acknowledges the tragic impact of the previous scene and begins the process of lifting the gloom established there.

121. He lives alone...housekeeper: The description is reminiscent of Knemon in *Old Cantankerous*. Both are antisocial towards their families and maintain households far below the standards expected. Both in fact exhibit traits of character that cause them to exist outside normal human society.

131-7. when he realised...today: The lines serve a double purpose:

1) They provide confirmation of Chairestratos' good nature not only through his willingness to take the girl into his household and to rear her no differently from his own daughter, but also through his generosity in providing for her future by means of a marriage and a dowry out of his own pocket.

2) They signal a strong contrast with the behaviour of Smikrines, whose interest in the girl materialises only *after* she becomes a source of wealth and who is prepared to overturn a wedding scheduled for that very day.

135. a substantial dowry: lit. 2 talents (12,000 drachmas), a figure which recurs in the fragmentary lines after 320. It is a nice piece of coincidence that the dowry envisaged by Chairestratos equals in value the 600 gold coins brought back by Daos.

148. I'm called Chance: The goddess' delay in revealing her name contrasts strongly with Pan's early self-identification in *Old Cantankerous* (cf. Plautus' *The Pot of Gold, Casina, Cistellaria, The Rope, Trinummus*) and has been criticised by some commentators. It does, however, add an extra element of suspense until realisation that misidentification of the corpse and the fortuitous return of the young man just in time to foil the schemes of his uncle are guided by the same divine hand, one, moreover, which had become a potent factor in human calculations in the political and economic upheaval of the 4th century BC.

149. feathering my nest: lit. 'a lover of money', the same term as was translated 'Money-grubber' in 123. Smikrines' assertion, a direct contradiction of what Chance has just established, neatly highlights his tendency to confirm the truth by denying it. It has already been glimpsed at 85f. (see n. above); here a similar insistence upon what he has *not* done indicates the true centre of his thought-processes and his calculating nature.

153. They're always casting aspersions on me: The paranoia that also characterises Smikrines is no less essential to depiction of him as the play's ogre figure than is his greed. It forms in fact the basis of his refusal at 261ff. to give up his claim to the girl despite all Chairestratos' arguments and financial inducements.

160f. no one thinks of weddings...just arrived: The statement contains obvious irony since thoughts of marriage are what now occupy the old man's own thoughts. What makes matters worse is that despite realising this is an inappropriate moment, he is still prepared to force the question of marriage back to the forefront of attention.

164. You have every excuse for behaving like this: Daos' address to those inside not only covers his otherwise unmotivated entry but also demonstrates his humane concern for their grief, a further contrast with Smikrines' attitude which continues when the two are brought into contact.

170f. the lawful heir of all my property: There is a problem here. It is the natural inference from the similarity of Smikrines' schemes against Kleostratos' sister and Chairestratos' daughter that his relationship to them is the same and that Smikrines, Chairestratos and Kleostratos' father were in consequence the offspring of the same father. By Attic law this would result in Smikrines' estate passing on his death without issue to his brothers equally in the first instance, or to their offspring if any brother predeceased (Harrison p. 143ff.), i.e., Kleostratos would share Smikrines' estate with Chairestratos. Has Menander, therefore, blundered in making the old man advance this claim, or does the emphasis upon Kleostratos have any special significance? Some have suggested it is a deliberate sham on Smikrines' part to prevent Chairestratos from inheriting, or a hint at Smikrines' previous intention to adopt his nephew and thus to make him his heir (Macdowell[2] p. 44f.). More likely it forms a cynical and hypocritical overstatement of regret at the death of his nephew at the very moment he begins to put into effect a plot to get his hands on the young man's estate. This same use of overstatement to bolster his own legal, though morally reprehensible, intentions resurfaces at 177 where the description 'giving the girl to God knows who' totally misrepresents the match between step-cousins for the sake of personal gain.

184f. the advice of some of my friends: These are doubtless imaginary friends, but provide further self-generated support for Smikrines' plans, similar to his later attempts to draw Daos into the plot at 187ff. By his contorted reasoning, offensive in its calculated self-interest, Smikrines has managed to convert his greed – at least to his own satisfaction – into action prescribed by law, supported by others, justified by the neglect he has supposedly suffered from his brother, and designed to wreak vengeance on Chairestratos in turn by denying him a share in Smikrines' own estate. Behind this final factor lies indeed the even worse prospect of the girl becoming mother to the old man's children.

191. 'know yourself': The words, inscribed on the temple of Apollo at Delphi, invite the reader not to contemplate his inner being but to recognise his mere humanity and to avoid claiming for himself privileges beyond those due to mortals; hence their relevance to a slave when he is urged to involve himself in a situation that is patently wrong. To escape becoming a pawn in Smikrines' plans Daos takes refuge in his servile status, with the limitations this imposes upon him, his foreign birth (which allows him to disavow Athenian laws and customs), and deference to the old man's superior status and knowledge (200ff., 208f.). Ironically it is also the slave who displays to a greater degree the loyalty and nobility usually associated with the free, and who in Act II shows by example the real disapproval that lies behind his forced neutral stance here. That this should additionally come from a Phrygian, typically regarded as cowardly and effeminate (as the Waiter indicates at 242, cf. Euripides' *Orestes* 1369ff., Tertullian *De Anima* 20 'comic writers mock the Phrygians as timid'), is an even greater surprise. As Sandbach[1] (p. 80) indicates, 'That one of this race should criticise Greek customs, and seem to have right on his side, is a pleasant paradox' (cf. Lombard p. 134ff.).

213. if there's no one at home?: Specifically Chairestratos, since he is effectively the only member of his household who has any real control over the wedding being planned.

213f. Chance, what a master...: The words form a deliberate reference to the play's guiding deity, this time in her reverse role as purveyor of bad luck. Daos' introduction of her here not only reminds the audience of the goddess' role in the action at the very point where Smikrines is about to embark on his scheme, but also allows the slave's subsequent activity to be represented as motivated by an element of natural self-interest (see further Zagagi[2]).

216ff. Cook: What is the purpose of the Cook's entry with all his inconsequential chatter at the end of the Act? Certainly it provides no bridge with events to come, as the introduction of Sikon and Getas does in *Old Cantankerous* Act II; nor is Sandbach's suggestion of a bridge, formed by a final reference to the marriage before Smikrines' action in Act II, particularly convincing. Rather than being prospective the introduction of the character seems in fact to look back to what has already occurred, providing at the end of the Act a more comic counterbalance to the tragic solemnity with which it opened, a counterbalance that is also ironically the product of that tragedy. So for instance, the complaint about his lack of success in securing engagements that do not collapse about his ears repeats in comic terms the effect Kleostratos' supposed death has on his family (8ff.), while the incongruity of 'Now a corpse arrives from Lycia' makes light of both the death itself and the gruesome description of the corpse given by Daos (71f.). The comedy-from-tragedy theme is further underlined by inversion of several stock topics associated with the cook character-type: instead of arriving at his employer's house (*Old Cantankerous* 393ff., Plautus' *The Pot of Gold* 280ff., *Casina* 720ff., *The Merchant* 714ff., *Pseudolus* 790ff.) we see him leaving; instead of boasting about his culinary skills, we hear his complaints. Only the abuse directed at his assistant for failing to take advantage of the situation (cf. Plautus' *The Pot of Gold* 322, 432ff., *Casina* 721ff., *Pseudolus* 850ff.) marks the conventional theme of culinary theft, though even here Menander inserts irony in his use of the common jibe 'temple-robber' (227 translated by Miller as 'You useless object') in a context where it is the *failure* to rob that lies at the centre of his complaint.

230. Sea-Green Incorruptible: lit. 'Aristeides', a soldier-politician in the period 490-70 BC whose reputation for honesty became proverbial.

233. Waiter: Does the waiter contribute anything new, or does he merely provide an extension of the comedy inherent in the cook character into even more farcical regions? Certainly, his macho self-regard allows introduction of the standard joke about Phrygians (in contrast to the use Daos himself made of his origins) and produces a brief comic counterpoint to the dejection of the cook.

Act II

The action that follows the choral interlude brings with it both a resumption and an intensification of the situation outlined in the earlier dialogue between Smikrines and Daos. For instance, we see resumption in the fact that the old man has by now put into effect his decision to halt the marriage planned between Chaireas and Kleostratos' sister, and is set on its replacement with another, less equal, match. Intensification comes in the now overt disapproval of such a match, this time by a free man, Chairestratos, which confirms the moral correctness of what had previously come incongruously, and in more muted terms, from a Phrygian slave. At the same time, Chairestratos' disapproval also allows repetition of Smikrines' own reaction to the situation: the paranoid feeling of neglect and conspiracy against him which justifies in his own mind the stand he takes on strict application of the law, but which merely serves in fact to underline his chief interest in the affair – profit. The obsession with his own rights on the part of Smikrines, and the havoc it wreaks upon the young couple involved, is further highlighted by the presence of Chaireas on stage throughout the dialogue (Frost p. 28).

255. I'm older than you: On this, Smikrines bases his prior claim to the girl and, as technical head of the whole family, his ability to overrule any arrangements made by Chairestratos.

272f. I can be brought to court...property?: The estate which devolved to an heiress did not become her property but was held in trust by her husband for their offspring. If Smikrines agrees to Chairestratos' proposal, therefore, and takes his nephew's estate but allows the marriage of the girl and Chaireas to go ahead, he becomes liable to later prosecution, following the birth of a male child, who would automatically become legal heir to Kleostratos' estate. To Smikrines' twisted thinking, of course, no amount of assurance from Chairestratos can make up for the insecurity of possession he would feel in such circumstances.

279-83: Like 262f., the lines echo the details given by Chance at 128-36, presenting the audience with an effective contrast, filled with comic irony, between Chairestratos' growing despondency and the goddess' earlier assurance that all would turn out well. In addition to their retrospective relevance, however, the old man's musings also foreshadow future events, as his wish for death becomes an element in Daos' plot and the reference to Kleostratos marrying Chairestratos' daughter points to the double betrothal mentioned at 521 in the highly fragmentary remains of Act V.

284ff. Chaireas: The young man's lament with its serious tone, its address to Kleostratos and its emphasis upon shattered dreams, forms yet another mirror-image, this time for Daos' monologue with which the play began. Despite the relevance of the young man for establishing the pathos of the plot, however, his actual role is remarkably meagre. He had, for instance, no part to play in the previous dialogue between the two old men, and once Daos enters, his contribution amounts to no more than three brief interventions (347, 375, 376-9). Why is this? Arnott[4] p.6 suggests a momentary lapse on the part of the playwright, but its cause may instead be that the young man's portrayal depends more on what he represents than on what he does: a victim whose fate lies in the hands of others.

300. You can't just lie there: Collapse as the result of despair, fore-shadowed at 282f., now becomes the cue for, and the means of, foiling Smikrines' plans. Stage action at this point, however, has been variously envisaged. Least likely is the suggestion that the collapse took place on stage, since this would seriously detract from the dramatic impact of Chaireas' monologue. Of the remaining scenarios there is little to choose between Daos' opening remarks being directed via the open door to Chairestratos behind the scene, or being delivered altogether off stage before the slave enters in order to summon Chaireas' help (cf. Frost p. 28ff.). That Chairestratos, on whom the ploy depends, must appear before the audience, despite his present state, is in fact no more illogical than the appearance of Knemon was at *Old Cantankerous* 909. Moreover, the old man's ability to describe himself in the stock terms of comic distress (305ff.) prevents the audience from taking his condition too seriously and enables him to assume a more active part in the ensuing dialogue than his stepson.

310. Did you say *marry*?: This is an illogical question in view of Smikrines' declaration at 185f., but is inserted partly for its emphatic effect and partly to draw Daos into a situation where he is the only character capable of taking control. In this way Menander achieves a reversal of role for him, just as he makes the music-girl Habrotonon assume responsibility for managing the plot in *The Arbitration* and turns the soldiers Polemon and Thrasonides into helpless lovers in *The Rape of the Locks* and *The Man She Hated*. Yet though Daos begins to take on the mantle of the cunning slave so familiar from Roman comedy, he is not yet the sole manager of the intrigue the type was later to become. Instead, both Chairestratos and Chaireas have a definite contribution to make: the former by deciding who will be let in on the plot, the latter in procuring a friend to play the doctor. This inclusion of father and stepson may be due in part to the as yet unrealised full potential of the slave character, and in part to the need to avoid an excessive discrepancy between the role Daos

106

is called upon to play here and his more sombre role in Act I.

327. He'll be a poor judge of reality: A necessary foundation for future developments. So far, apart from his paranoid view of others' behaviour and attitudes towards him, Smikrines has not been totally lacking in astuteness so far as his own advantage is concerned. Daos now proposes to use that astuteness against him, but in order that the broad humour involved in this remains credible, he here converts the old man's preoccupation with self-interest into a weakness, explaining in advance his inability to see through the blatant trickery that will be used against him. In the same way the part Chairestratos is called upon to play is neatly prepared for by the description of him as having 'a bitter, melancholic side' (338f.).

328f. So what...you like: The lines are designed as a prompt that provides the semblance of dialogue without the substance, and to present the plot in easily grasped stages: first the illness (330-42), then the death (343-6), and finally the inheritance (348-52).

348. Then *your* daughter becomes an heiress: This constitutes the reason for making Chaireas no more than a step-son: any closer blood relationship would automatically have allowed him to succeed to the estate himself. Daos' plot has, however, one potentially fatal flaw: it may deflect Smikrines' attention from Kleostratos' sister for the moment, but it cannot prevent for ever the old man's scheme to marry her. Once he realises he has been duped over Chairestratos' daughter, there will be nothing to stop him resurrecting his original plan, even to the extent of forcing a divorce upon the girl and Chaireas if they have subsequently married (see, however, MacDowell[2] p. 49f.). It is for this reason, as well as to establish the play within the ambit of the comic genre, that Kleostratos must eventually return in order to resume his role as his sister's legal guardian, able to dispose of her to a more suitable husband.

350f. a larger fortune: lit. 'about 60 talents' (360,000 drachmas), a far larger sum than the four talents (24,000 drachmas) stated in the Greek text to be the value of Kleostratos' estate, including the booty brought back from Lycia. The enormity of the discrepancy is clearly an instance of comic overkill designed to leave Smikrines no option but to indulge his greed to the full.

358. fix seals on doors: While locking things up might deter casual pilfering, it provides no defence against use of a duplicate key. Attachment of a marked seal, on the other hand, unmistakably shows if there has been any attempt to gain unauthorised access to property.

362ff.: Reference in the fragmentary remains of these lines to exacting twice the amount points to the penalty someone convicted of theft was forced to pay: twice the value of the stolen goods. This suggests that Daos' plan involved Smikrines seizing Chairestratos' estate and then being prosecuted by his brother after a miraculous recovery.

372f. 'The wolf's jaws...hungry': The analogy is highly apposite: Smikrines will be electrified by the expectation of such an enormous inheritance, while those around him enjoy the realisation of his inevitable disappointment.

375. A bit of a quack?: The description reflects the conventional depiction of doctors on the comic stage. The fact that Chaireas has to bring in a blatant impostor is not an otiose detail but allows the introduction of even broader humour as he shamelessly hoodwinks Smikrines and thus confirms Daos' forecast at 326f. In carrying out the deception, the wig and stick were doubtless needed to age Chaireas' friend; the cloak, of the same high-quality as worn by Sostratos in *Old Cantankerous* (257), suggests the affluence of success (cf. Alexis' *Mandragorizomene* fr. 142 in which a character complains that home-grown doctors are spurned, while those speaking in a foreign accent command respect simply because of the dialect).

385f. Let the rest...dead: Though Chairestratos could rely upon his immediate family to fall in with the pretence, the rest of the household is made to suffer the same misapprehension as Smikrines in order to render their reactions the more convincing. Within this, however, Chairestratos envisages a self-deprecating element of comic incongruity.

Act III

391ff.: Behind the tortuous logic of Smikrines' complaints lie multiple levels of irony:

1) While suspicions of conspiracy against him continue to reflect the paranoia within his thinking, they do for once represent reality. This is not, however, the reality the old man supposes, which serves merely to justify his rejection of any feelings of altruism.

2) Smikrines' misinterpretation of Daos' motives in preparing the inventory – an attempt to minimise Kleostratos' estate – not only allows him to indulge in misplaced and premature self-congratulation but foreshadows, in fact, a more successful attempt to deny him the estate altogether.

3) Though the old man's appreciation of Daos' tricky character puts him on his guard against the slave, his greed imposes upon him a blindness which nevertheless causes him to fall victim to Daos' plotting, for all its blatant histrionics.

415. Will he never stop?: The question underlines the comic incongruity between preparations for delivering the news and the news itself, as Daos rushes about the stage in mock despair, apparently unaware of

Smikrines' presence, yet with the audience knowing full well that the whole show is being put on for his benefit (see further Turner[1] p. 133).

433f. If they see me...: The failure of the old man to follow the others inside is motivated primarily by technical considerations, i.e., to avoid an empty stage, as in the case of Sikon at *Old Cantankerous* 639ff., but is well motivated in dramatic terms by 360f. and very much in keeping with Smikrines' calculating nature.

456. Come over here: Damage to the text here makes restoration uncertain. What remains consists of 'you, you', 'you summon back', 'yes...over here, away from the door'. It may, however, represent an instance of Menander inserting a momentary hint of danger to the plot – the suggestion that Smikrines' urgent cry betokens he has seen through the sham (cf. *Old Cantankerous* 784 n.) – before directing the dialogue into even more farcical regions as the doctor begins playing on Smikrines' own susceptibilities.

Act IV

If Act IV of *The Shield* follows Menandrean technique already seen elsewhere, the situation developed in previous Acts will now have been taken to its crisis point before its inevitable resolution. What form the point of crisis actually assumed we cannot tell since virtually all of Acts IV and V is lost. Resolution of the plot, on the other hand, is more open to restoration, both as a result of extant remains and the demands of the plot itself. Before the dialogue given in the translation, the papyrus preserves the beginnings of some 22 lines and indicates that one of the speakers involved was Smikrines. As to the contents of the lines, all we can safely say is that news of Chairestratos' death reaches his brother, who may then begin the process of transferring his attentions to his other niece by betrothing Kleostratos' sister to someone else, presumably Chaireas. Following this the stage is emptied of characters in readiness for the return of Kleostratos himself and the portrayal of what Goldberg[2] p. 26 calls a 'gatekeeper scene' in which a character returning after an absence has his way barred by another. (cf. Plautus' *Amphityro* 292ff., *The Ghost* 446ff. The device has its origins in tragedy: Aeschylus' *Libation Bearers* 652ff., Euripides' *Helen* 435ff., and Old Comedy: Aristophanes' *Clouds* 131ff., *Frogs* 35ff.) Like Menelaos in Euripides' play, Kleostratos' initial optimism wilts before the news of Chairestratos' supposed death (a comic counterpart to earlier announcements) and Daos' unwelcoming attitude. Before long, however, the scene changes to one of recognition, which immediately ushers in Kleostratos' main function as *deus ex machina*. His very return solves all the difficulties so far built up, removes any possiblility of Smikrines' claiming the young man's sister, and enables Chairestratos to abandon his pretended death, leaving Smikrines with all his plans in ruins. (For detailed, if speculative, restoration of the fragments see Arnott[4].)

Act V

The remains of the final Act consist of no more than the ends of some 29 lines set in the lively trochaic tetrameter metre, suggesting an atmosphere of pure comedy. As the translation indicates, the contents of what remains hint at a description of the happiness caused by Kleostratos' return and preparations for a double wedding. Thereafter it would seem that Smikrines arrives on stage still obsessed with his plans for marriage and willing to give Chaireas what he wants, a fitting point at which, perhaps, to introduce his well deserved discomfiture (cf. Arnott[4]).

The Sikyonian

Act I

While it is possible to gain some overall understanding of *The Sikyonian*'s basic plot, founded as it is on the standard themes of lost children and rivalry in love, its extant remains present us with difficulties that go far beyond anything so far encountered. The fact, for instance, that our principal source of information (part of a papyrus roll written in the second half of the 3rd century BC) was subsequently incorporated into three separate mummy cases itself poses problems for the reassembling of scenes. Added to this is the accident that what we possess comes largely from Acts IV & V, which means that for the most part we have the solutions to problems developed in earlier Acts, but often no way of telling exactly how those problems arose or were represented. The same is true of passing references to characters and events in the remains of earlier Acts. What bearing, if any, these had on subsequent action is often a mystery. Take, for example, the Boeotian mentioned in 134 and the debt owed to him. Does he constitute mere local colouring or does he have a role to play in later scenes as some have supposed? Under what circumstances did Moschion become acquainted with Philoumene and Dromon, and what prompts the plan that Theron attempts to put into action in Act V? Does the fragmentary Greek text at 52ff., with its mention of a witness, provide any hint of such a plan? Does Theron, in fact, achieve the hoped-for marriage with Malthake referred to at 144? Even the title of the play is a source of contention, since the papyrus and a wall painting in Ephesus which depicts an otherwise unidentified scene in the action give instead the plural form *The Sikyonians*. Further complications arise from our uncertainty as to who it is who speaks in some scenes, the result of textual damage which is often, and inevitably, masked in the translation. Is it, for instance, Blepes who interacts with Smikrines from 150, or is the altercation with which the Act opens such that it demands a change of personnel at 169? And who exactly threatens arrest at 272ff.? Commentators are in no way united in their conclusions, tentative as such conclusions often are. As a result restraint becomes an

essential watchword in any attempt to restore dramatic action and motivation in scenes we either do not possess or in which the imperfect
survival of evidence results in only a partial picture. To do otherwise, to
set one hypothesis upon another in an ever widening tangle of possibility,
is simply to construct a house of cards that will convince no one but
ourselves, and collapse at the first opportunity (see further Sandbach[1]
p. 634ff.).

1ff. A God: As Miller n. 4 observes, the quality of the information
provided by the prologue, like the appeal for the audience's favour in 24
(cf. *Old Cantankerous* 45f.), points to a divine speaker in these lines,
even if the identity of the figure involved remains totally unknown.

[the pirates]: Not given in the Greek text, though their identity had
doubtless been established earlier in the prologue and they are specifically mentioned in 357. There too we find reference to Halai as the
location of the kidnap: either Halai Araphrenides on the NE coast of
Attica, between Marathon and Brauron, or Halai Aixonides, between the
Piraeus and Sunion. Philoumene would then have been taken across the
Aegean to Caria in SW Asia Minor where, as in the case of Lycia in *The
Shield*, there was regular employment to be gained by mercenary soldiers
such as the Sikyonian who bought her.

4. the old lady: This is probably the girl's nurse, since we know from
355 that Philoumene was four when she was abducted. Though the old
woman has no further role to play in the extant action, her insertion here
may have foreshadowed the means by which Kichesias learned of his loss
later in the prologue.

13ff. The man who's...and rich, too: Identification of the soldier
with Stratophanes is nowhere guaranteed by the text, but is at least suggested on a *prima facie* level by the claim at 226, 'I've brought up this
girl from childhood'. Some, however, have emphasised the age difference this would create between Stratophanes and Philoumene, who
must by now be of marriageable age and therefore at least sixteen, while
her purchaser was already an established military figure twelve years
earlier. As Sandbach[1] p. 637 observes, however, the fact that Stratophanes' mother died at a great age (126) itself indicates he is no stripling,
and the resulting age difference would be no more regarded as untoward
in ancient Greek terms than it is in modern.

119ff.: For all its ostensibly expository nature and similarity with *Old
Cantankerous* 50ff. the scene between Stratophanes, Theron and Pyrrhias
belongs not to Act I but rather to the closing sections of Act III. We know
this because it is directly linked in the papyrus with the entry of Smikrines which comes after the choral interlude, and since the Greek letter

Eta (H = 700) appears in the margin of what is line 151 of our translation, this suggests on the analogy of other Menandrean plays that Act IV has just begun. In *Old Cantankerous*, for instance, Act IV opens at 620; in *The Arbitration* it occurs at 714, and in *The Rape of the Locks* at 708 (textual factors, however, prevent total precision in these last two figures). As for its dramatic content the scene is marked by a rapidity of interplay between characters that is underpinned by the trochaic tetrameter metre in which it is set. Elsewhere this often serves to bolster the comic atmosphere of a scene, though this is clearly not the case here any more than it was at *Old Cantankerous* 708ff.

123f. So why on earth...top speed, too?: Despite the slave's hasty entrance, reminiscent of the running slave character of later Roman comedy, the six lines actually taken to introduce him not only serve to prepare the audience for the news he brings, through such descriptive details as 'down in the mouth', but also enable him to launch directly into a series of serious revelations, without the need for any preliminary exchange of greetings that might otherwise have diminished the tension of the encounter (Frost p. 119, cf. Euripides' *Hippolytos* 1151f., *Phoenissai* 1332ff., Aristophanes' *Acharnians* 1069f., Plautus' *The Merchant* 598ff.).

126. Died last year: The information succinctly indicates that Stratophanes has been away from his home in Sikyon for some considerable time and thus lays the foundation for the situation soon to be outlined by Pyrrhias.

131ff. On your death-bed...family: The form assumed by this portentous pronouncement in the Greek points to its use as a maxim, which Sandbach[1] observes strikes something of a false note. The woman's death-bed concern for her son contrasts strongly indeed with the unspoken assumption that until that moment the identity of Stratophanes' true parents had been a well guarded secret. It is, in fact, Theron's use of such statements, his tendency to inquisitiveness and to agree (122, and probably such reactions in the fragmentary section before 119 as: 'Good!', 'It's my opinion now', 'Yes, by God'), together with the self-interest behind the wish for Stratophanes to get his girl (145), that help to categorise him as a parasite (cf. Charisios in *Old Cantankerous*). Even his name, which translates as Hunter, seems appropriate to the role.

135. a large sum of money: lit. 'many talents'. The significance of the debt lies in the threat it poses to Stratophanes' inheritance and to his person. Certainly in Attic law, the loser in such a case could be liable to seizure until the debt was paid, and for the purposes of the play Menander may well have assumed an identical legal position existed in Sikyon and Boeotia. Why, though, is the theme of the debt introduced at all except to prompt revelation of the soldier's true origins? As already mentioned, some early commentators saw a role for the Boeotian in causing Philoumene and Dromon, who technically count among Stratophanes' possessions, to seek the protection of the temple precinct (190ff.) and thus avoid seizure. Yet apart from the reference here, there is no mention of such a possible threat elsewhere in the extant text. Instead, as Sandbach[1] p.635 argues, what evidence there is points to the girl seeking protection through fear of her master (194), something already mentioned in the fragmentary line 97 ('she says she fears her foreign master') and perhaps a factor underlying Stratophanes' statement at 241 ('she has nothing to fear, at least from me'). This suggests, in fact, quite a different scenario: that Philoumene, aware of her original freeborn Athenian status and Stratophanes' love for her (254), seeks to preserve her virginity from the danger she imagines he poses to it.

142. tokens to prove your identity: The words point to the usual objective means of establishing the identity of a character who was exposed as a baby (cf. *The Arbitration*), or handed over to someone else, as here (cf. 280f.).

144. Lady of Athens: The goddess Athena, as the Greek text indicates. In dramatic terms, the wish that follows clearly foreshadows the ultimate aim of the play, a legal marriage between Stratophanes and Philoumene, whose citizen status already underlies the theme of kidnap. That Theron too gets his girlfriend is perhaps suggested by a reference in Pollux IV, 19 (if indeed it refers to Menander's play): 'The parasites (wear) black or grey, except in *The Sikyonian* (where he wears) white since the parasite intends to get married'. What status such an ostensibly formal marriage would have, however, remains obscure. Malthake's relationship to the soldier is suggestive of her being both his mistress and his housekeeper. The instructions to oversee the transfer of property to the house of Stratophanes' new-found parents at 386ff., for instance, are reminiscent of Chrysis' return to dramatic focus in *The Girl from Samos* 730 (cf. fr. 1 below). Such a role, however, would clearly be at variance with her proving to be freeborn Athenian and it is questionable whether Theron, who is himself perhaps a poor Athenian, could be shown accepting a soldier's cast-off.

146. No more talking: The peremptory tone of Stratophanes' command (cf. 141, 145f.) characterises him as someone accustomed to giving orders, and thus fully able to thwart Theron's attempt to discover the contents of the papers brought by Pyrrhias. In this way Menander ends the Act with an element of mystery and tension that remains until the reported revelations of 246ff (see Sandbach[1], Frost p. 119).

Act IV

If *The Sikyonian* is constructed on the analogy of those Menandrean plays already studied, we might expect to find developed in its fourth Act a final manifestation of whatever obstacles stand in the way of the obligatory happy ending, followed by their resolution. In so far as Stratophanes' discovery of his true parents vindicates his claim to Athenian citizenship, this would indeed seem to be the case, since it automatically opens up the prospect of marriage with Philoumene, whose own Athenian status doubtless figured in previous Acts. Likewise, it resolves the rivalry over the girl between the soldier and Moschion. Such rivalry, in fact, so vividly described in the narrative that forms the core of Act IV, undergoes a twofold development, with Moschion's efforts first neutralised by the assembly and then rendered void by the discovery that he is Stratophanes' brother. Why, though, is Philoumene's discovery of her own father not likewise inserted into the Act? Does its relegation to a later stage signal Menander's deliberate variation of his basic plot structure so as not to overcrowd Act IV, or does the ease with which the discovery is effected (reminiscent of Pamphile's recognition in *The Arbitration*) suggest that its inevitability had already been signalled and it was not therefore a major point of contention in the play? As such, might it serve instead as an element in the discomfiture of a troublesome character (Theron), something that is a recurrent theme of fifth Acts?

While the central section of the Act, the description of the assembly, presents few major problems for interpretation, the opening scene or scenes as set out by the papyrus prove more troublesome. How many characters, for instance, are actually involved and who are they? That one is called Blepes is virtually certain from the insertion of the name in 188, but is he to be identified with the figure who enters with Smikrines at the beginning? And is the name Smikrines, with its connotations of tight-fistedness, as in *The Arbitration* and *The Shield*, the correct interpretation of the letters *Sm* which occur in 156, and are the only hint of the name in the whole play? Who indeed is Smikrines? Despite the lack of any objective indication within the text, editors have unanimously identified him with Stratophanes' father. This, after all, allows development of significant dramatic irony as he hears of a dispute between two figures who turn out to be his own sons, unaware that for all his 'oligarchical' sentiments his family is to benefit from the 'democratic' decision of the assembly to protect the girl's interests (cf. Smikrines in *The Arbitration*, MacCary[2] p. 311ff.).

At 167, the dispute which marked the entry of the two characters reaches a climax of mutual scorn sufficient for some commentators to suggest that one of them leaves, to be immediately replaced by Blepes (Frost p. 120f., cf. p. 14, where he points to similar insults at the point of departure in *The Arbitration* 376, and *The Rape of the Locks* 526). Such a scenario, even involving the introduction of a totally unheralded incident, is not, in fact, beyond the bounds of possibility, especially if taken as parodying tragic messenger speeches, which were often injected with equal abruptness (Sandbach[1] p. 647). There are, however, undoubted pointers towards continuity of stage personnel and dramatic advantages to be gained from it:

1) The criticism of Smikrines at 156 as 'a real dyed-in-the-wool old élitist' (lit. 'oligarch') finds a parallel in Blepes' probable description of himself at 182 as 'a democrat'.

2) By linking Smikrines' criticism of the man 'who weeps and pleads' (151f.) with the tears shed by Stratophanes in 219f. (partially restored in the Greek), his opening speech becomes not an element in some abstract discussion but an ironic condemnation of a son whose behaviour is subsequently fully vindicated.

161. but I might be of some use...: The statement is no more than a speculative restoration of text based on Smikrines' response. This whole section indeed suffers from damage to the papyrus affecting 159-82, 192-6, 211-35.

172. I'm listening: lit. 'We want to hear'. Though there is adequate evidence for the use of plurals in the context of individual characters elsewhere in Menander, its insertion here and at 175, lit. 'Tell us all', injects yet another point of uncertainty into a scene already beset by problems.

176f. I happened...no indeed...: Despite the fragmentary nature of the Greek text (lit. 'I happened to be coming, not ... no by Zeus, nor...') commentators have seen an allusion here to the opening of the messenger speech in Euripides' *Orestes* 866ff. ('I happened to be coming into town from the country'). That such closeness of phrasing is no mere accident is suggested by:

1) the further echo that occurs at 182 ('part of the backbone of the country' lit. 'who alone preserve the country') which mirrors exactly *Orestes* 920;

2) the depiction of similar situations in the two plays, a debate before a popular assembly. (In the Euripidean play this involves both Orestes and Electra, who are on trial for the murder of their mother Clytemnestra, an instance of the playwright deglamourising the myth just as Menander goes one stage further by applying the theme to a dispute over a girl.)

116

3) the fact that Menander has chosen to set the incident in the form of a quasi-tragic messenger speech, involving greater strictness of metre than was normal in comedy, the absence of interruptions that usually characterise his long speeches before a stage audience (cf. 196 n., *The Shield* 22ff., *The Man She Hated* 284ff.), and the motif of the suppliant, itself common in tragedy (Aeschylus' *Suppliant Maidens*, *Eumenides*, Sophocles' *Oedipus at Colonus*, Euripides' *Children of Heracles* and *Suppliants*; see further Arnott[4] p. xlif., [7] Turner[1] p. 22f. and Katsouris[1] p. 29-54 who provides a detailed comparison of the speeches).

182. I'm a democrat: Though the term is the result of textual restoration, it is perhaps preferable to the alternative, 'workman', not least since the speaker's previous description of himself as '[thriving] on other people's troubles ... a terror on a jury', his greetings to all and sundry, and his claim to represent 'the backbone of the country' all point to democratic sympathies.

184f. sharing out a skinny little bullock: The theme of the sacrificial bull is less common than that of the skinny sheep, which might be the offering of an individual (cf. *Old Cantankerous* 393ff. n.). It does, however, occur again at Theocritus *Idyll* IV, 20ff.: 'The bull too, the tawny one, is certainly a thin specimen. The descendants of Lampriades should get such a one when the villagemen are sacrificing to Hera'.

188. Blepes: The name represents a slight emendation of the papyrus text, but is the only viable possibility.

194. ...her present guardian is threatening her safety: Who is referred to here? The evidence of the extant text (including the fragmentary line at 97 'she says she fears her foreign master') points most immediately to Stratophanes, despite the attempts of some to reintroduce the Boeotian at this point (see above, 135 n.).

196f. we all roared out ... Athenian': The cry of the crowd indicates not only that Philoumene's claim to be Athenian figured in the missing section of Dromon's speech, but also that it was accepted by them. It is notable how in a speech unrelieved by Menander's usual technique of interruption from another character, he is nevertheless able to introduce variety by directly quoting those who took part in the assembly.

200. a young lad: Moschion, who first appears on stage at 272 in the extant text. That he must have been seen before this, however, is suggested by the lack of further identification here, and the probability that the conversation between Dromon and Stratophanes mentioned in 207 was portrayed on stage (see n. below). From the outset, the details given of him conspire to damn his cause: his pale face indicative of lechery according to Aristotle, his shaven chin a sign of effeminacy (cf. 'pansy' lit. 'shaven' 264), the attempted secrecy of his conversation with Dromon, and the impression that his aim is seduction (210). At the same time, the fact that Moschion will emerge as Stratophanes' brother by the end of the play rules out a portrayal of unrelieved blackness, hence, perhaps, his embarrassment and withdrawal at 208, which presupposes he knows he is doing wrong, and the description of him in 209 as being not totally beyond redemption.

207. when he was talking just now to his master: Though there is no obvious sign of such a scene in the text, it may lurk among the tattered fragments of dialogue at 72ff., where the name Dromon occurs at 78, and at 82 a character (Dromon?) is chided for having ruined someone's chances (an aside by Moschion?). Similarly, the address formula 'young man' in 108 may point to a role in monologue form (?) for Moschion himself, while at 102-5 comes a reference to a servant and the fact that the girl is of citizen birth. At all events, the fact that Stratophanes fails to recognise Moschion in the debate before the assembled crowd indicates that the young man's knowledge was gained by eavesdropping (Sandbach[1] p. 640).

215. a fine, upstanding man: lit. 'a very manly individual', in total contrast to the picture given of Moschion. The dichotomy is further underlined by (1) no attempt at secretive contact on the part of the soldier; (2) no embarrassment, even at his own emotional reaction to the sight of Philoumene; (3) the matter-of-fact attitude underlying his staccato statements in 236-9, which reinforces the impression of efficient generosity as he relinquishes any claim he may have had on the girl (cf. Syros' style of delivery in *The Arbitration* 294ff.); and (4) the approval his suggested course of action wins from the crowd in 245.

241. at least from me: Like the later reference at 255f. ('And don't let any of my rivals ... before her father appears') the words are doubtless directed against Moschion for all their generalised phrasing.

260ff. 'Are you asking me...': Despite the crowd's favourable response to Stratophanes' own claim to citizenship, there has been nothing so far that provides them with any objective evidence of its validity. To escape this logical difficulty, Menander raises the possibility of deception by the soldier, but in a manner that backfires on Moschion through the impression of partisan interference, and leads readily to rejection of his charge. Thus, while fulfilling the demands of logic, the accusation does nothing to hold up the flow of the action for more than a few moments. Instead, it allows the narrative to end on a note of dramatic tension.

264. Then there was confused shouting – : This is little more than a stage direction altogether absent from the Greek, which merely quotes the insults traded. How many are involved in the exchange and who they are remains unresolved. The least likely scenario includes a role for Stratophanes, whose address to the girl at 267 shows none of the agitation we might otherwise have expected. If this is the case, jibes directed at the soldier by Moschion would also seem to be excluded. This leaves the possibility of either an exchange restricted entirely to the crowd or one between the crowd and Moschion, which is the impression given by the translation. Difficulties of interpreting the Greek, however, prevent any certain decision.

272ff. Kidnappers! I arrest you – : The scene which now erupts unheralded onto the stage presents yet further problems of interpretation, caused by the total absence within the papyrus of any objective information as to who the speakers are. Again, no solution so far offered is totally free from difficulty. Commentators generally hold that New Comedy followed Greek Tragedy in restricting itself to three speaking actors, which readily accounts for (1) the fact that no extant scene requires more than three speaking parts; (2) apparently premature exits for some characters in order to change costume and mask; and (3) the practice of speaking characters putting words into the mouth of a fourth figure played by a mute (*The Rape of the Locks* Act V, *The Man She Hated* 208ff.; see further Sandbach[1] p. 16ff., Frost p. 2f.). Since it would therefore seem contrary to convention for both Smikrines and Blepes to leave the stage and be replaced by Moschion and Stratophanes with no apparent opportunity for a change of costume, there is some attraction in the suggestion of Lloyd-Jones[1] p. 152 that Smikrines remains on stage and is then threatened with arrest (together with Moschion, in view of the plural 'you' and 'us') by the newly arrived Stratophanes. The charge would presumably be that they are attempting to gain possession of Philoumene. As Sandbach[1] p. 659f. demonstrates, however:

1) Until Philoumene's claim to citizen status was revealed in the missing section before 194, any attempt by Smikrines or Moschion to secure her, certainly by purchase, could not be illegal.

2) Since Moschion's apparent designs on the girl have already been thwarted, any further action against him is otiose.

3) Until his own citizen status has been established, Stratophanes is in no position to threaten any Athenian with arrest.

4) It would be difficult to apply the term 'lad' to Stratophanes at 274 unless it was being used ironically, since it was normally associated with the 18-21 age-group. On the other hand, it is found in the context of Moschion at 200.

5) There is no evidence for such a scenario in the text's extant remains.

In view of such objections, other commentators see little alternative to a complete change of stage personnel, with Moschion, smarting from his recent discomfiture and still convinced that Stratophanes is intent on obtaining Philoumene by deception, attempting to arrest the soldier (and perhaps Theron, if the plurals again have any force. Certainly, the fact that Theron knows the whereabouts of his master at 365ff. suggests he must have some role in the present scene). Yet how does this fit in with the three-actor rule? One solution calls for the slow exit of Smikrines, allowing the actor who played Blepes to reappear as either Moschion or Stratophanes. Yet not only would such an exit be without parallel in Menander, its undoubted awkwardness could so easily have been avoided by a brief exit-monologue from the old man, similar to that from Sostratos at *Old Cantankerous* 381ff., or from Stratophanes at 385ff. in the present play (see further Frost p. 121ff.). One final pointer to Moschion and Stratophanes as the characters comes in the events portrayed when the text resumes at 280. Again the papyrus provides no indication of speaker, except what can be gleaned from the actual words spoken: the reference to a husband in 306 of the Greek text, to a brother in 309f., and the name Moschion in 309 (the address 'father' in 309 exists only through restoration). This is enough, however, to suggest the involvement of Stratophanes, together with his father and mother, in what is ostensibly the recognition scene prepared for by 249ff. If indeed only a single column of some twenty lines separated this from what went before, the very proximity of events would suggest continuity of theme, but of this we cannot be certain.

Act V

Though it suffers from considerable textual damage, the opening of the Act continues to display Menander's skill in character portrayal as Theron lures Kichesias on an ever-lengthening stroll, presumably in the hope of building up a rapport with the old man that will then make Theron's request for cooperation all the more difficult to turn down. What remains of this fragmentary section yields the sense: '*Kichesias*: What's so important between us that it seems worth all this walking about you've taken me on, forever asking me to go a little further?...'.

344ff. Did you really think...: To facilitate understanding of the scene, commentators point to the analogy of Plautus' *Poenulus* (*Little Carthaginian*) 1087ff., in which the slave Milphio attempts to persuade the old man Hanno to pose as the father of two girls in the clutches of a pimp. In this way he hopes to secure their freedom, since one of them is the girlfriend of his young master. Unbeknown to Milphio, however, Hanno is indeed the girls' long-lost father and when he recalls their loss, the slave thinks he is merely playing the required part. Into the present instance Menander injects the additional factor of Kichesias, who must already be known to the audience for the scene to work, rejecting an earlier plan of Theron's. The substance of this, though lost in one of the gaps, perhaps required the old man to provide (false) evidence that Kichesias was Philoumene's father (cf. Sandbach[1] p. 663). Such a scenario has the advantage of portraying Kichesias as an essentially moral character in his refusal to participate in perjury. It also demonstrates that by misconstruing the stand taken by the old man as an assumption of Kichesias' character, Theron effectively loses control of the situation, and in the audience's eyes becomes a dupe to his own scheming. Why, though, if the identity of Philoumene's father is apparently known by now, does Theron persist with so tortuous a course of action? One possible answer may lie in the portrayal of him elsewhere in the play as inherently devious, someone for whom the obvious course of action is never the one adopted, and a figure whose unnecessary complexities of manoeuvre make possible the development of considerable dramatic irony. Equally, it may be no more than a desperate attempt to speed up the soldier's marriage, an attempt which is rendered otiose by the ease of recognition when it comes.

346f. Kichesias Skambonides: The word-play produced by repetition of the name in the Greek text here and at 349f. is given further emphasis by identical location within their respective lines. Both instances, in fact, straddle their verses, with Kichesias at the end of one and Skambonides at the beginning of the next, each a significant position in poetic terms (cf. the prologue to *Old Cantankerous*. Note the line number 350 is incorrectly sited in the translation; it belongs instead beside the second reference to Kichesias Skambonides). Further instances of such significant positioning within the scene include Halai at the beginning of 355, Dromon in 356 and Kichesias (translated 'sir') in 364, while occupying the final position in lines we find Stratophanes in 365, 377, 381, Kichesias in 368, Dromon in 371, 374, Malthake in 386, and Donax in 385.

352f. you're short and snub-nosed: Theron's observation of the similarity between his victim and Kichesias further highlights the irony of his scheme, a scheme with which he is so bound up he cannot grasp the obvious inference of what he sees or is told; hence the climactic 'He's a great chap!' (360) immediately before the entry of Dromon bursts the bubble of misapprehension.

367. Still, I'll go and get Stratophanes: Despite the partial recovery of Kichesias, whose fainting fit underlines the poignancy of the loss he had earlier described, it nevertheless remains necessary for Theron to leave in order to maintain the three-actor rule.

372. She's still a virgin: Dromon perceptively sees to the heart of Kichesias' previous question, drawing attention to the potential fate of a kidnapped girl being forced to become her owner's mistress, or worse, a prostitute in the power of a pimp. As it is, her virgin state both confirms the nobility of Stratophanes' behaviour and forms the preliminary to marriage.

375f. a poor, lonely old man: Why is Kichesias portrayed in this way? Is it, like the shock of discovery, to heighten the pathos of the scene? For the sentiment compare Philemon fr. 125 'How are you? – Don't ask. When you see an old man or woman, you can take it for granted they're in a bad way'.

377ff. Stratophanes, this is Philoumene's *father*!...: At the point where the two strands of the plot's love element are brought together, both the action and the dialogue undergo such a quickening of pace under the direction of Dromon as to appear almost forced. Stratophanes' attempt to broach the subject of marriage at 380f., for instance, is immediately cut short by the interruption of the slave, while Kichesias' part becomes relegated, ostensibly by his bewilderment, to a mere three words of blessing, and these not even addressed directly to the soldier.

382. let's go and get Philoumene: Like the words Stratophanes directed to his mother at 377, which were probably designed to indicate completion of the recognition and his parents' awareness of the situation, Dromon's instruction here (radically restored) seems designed more for technical than dramatic reasons – to remind the audience that Philoumene is for the moment in the care of the priestess (242, 269f.) and to signal her transfer to her father's house.

385ff. Donax!...: Why, after the extreme brevity of the meeting with Kichesias, is Stratophanes made to deal with the transfer of his belongings from one house to another at such length? Is it simply to cover the time needed for one of the actors who have just left to change into the costume and mask of Moschion? And why is Theron left behind in the lowly company of foreign slaves and donkey-drivers? Is it part of his 'reward' for earlier misdirected interference, or does it represent disappointment now, in preparation for eventual union with Malthake? A similar question of motivation surrounds the subsequent appearance of Moschion, whose monologue reveals little more than acceptance that his would-be love affair has failed. Might it be that such acceptance marks the first stage in his eventual absorption into the marriage celebrations as Best Man, a figure who traditionally accompanied the groom on the carriage which took the bride to her new home? Before that, is he first shown the error of his ways? We cannot tell, though this would be altogether appropriate on the analogy of Moschion in *The Rape of the Locks* and Clitipho in Terence's *The Self-Tormentor*.

387. the house next door – : The intervention of comic coincidence, ensuring in the present case that Stratophanes has set up home next door to his real parents.

405. Ladies and gentlemen: lit. 'Gentlemen' (cf. *Old Cantankerous* 194 n.).

Unassigned fragments

1. Photius, Suda: 'For he bought instead a lady's maid. The girl that he loved he didn't hand over to the woman here but raised her separately, as befits a freeborn person.'

   Though textual uncertainties exist within the fragment, these do not materially affect the sense. Sandbach[1] suggests it belongs to a lost section of the prologue and describes Stratophanes' treatment of Philoumene, whom he did not hand over to Malthake.

2. Stobaeus' *Eclogae* IV, 12, 4: 'The soldier's and the stranger's bearing appears open to reproach, so it seems.'

3. Photius: 'Once, Stratophanes, you had a simple little soldier's cloak and a single slave.'

4. Photius, Suda: ' A sailor comes ashore. He is judged to be an enemy. If he has any personal possessions, he is pressed into forced labour.'

5. Photius, Suda: 'A vile countenance and a wretched mind behind it.'

6. Stobaeus' *Eclogae* II, 33, 4: 'The choice of like-minded persons is most likely to bring harmony out of life's variety.' Attribution of this to *The Sikyonian* is no more than tentative.

The Man She Hated

Act I

As with *The Sikyonian*, the extant remains of *The Man She Hated* present considerable obstacles to any detailed appreciation of the dramatic action. To begin with, the fragments from which the play is pieced together come from nearly a dozen separate papyri, widely differing in their dates of production, and all suffering from extensive damage, so that attribution of lines and even the identity of characters within scenes become uncertain. Then again, though the surviving text is more evenly distributed throughout the play than was the case with *The Sikyonian* (we have in fact parts of all but Act II, which is represented only by odd words, phrases and half-lines), this also means that available information is spread more thinly, so that there remain vital aspects which are either vague or impossible to fathom (see further Sandbach[1] p. 438ff.).

A1ff. O Night...: The opening scene has affinities with its counterpart in *The Shield*:

1) Both are expository and contain an initial monologue which sets the atmosphere for what is to come, not only through its contents, but also through the application of stricter metrical rules than is normal for comedy.

2) Both outline a situation built upon misapprehension, suggesting that *The Man She Hated*, no less than *The Shield*, originally contained a deferred divine prologue, which revealed those otherwise unknown factors upon which the widespread injection of dramatic irony could be based.

Commentators have also pointed to the similarity, albeit distorted, between Thrasonides' predicament and the complaint of the lover shut out from the home of his beloved, common in later literature (Goldberg[2] p. 51f., Katsouris[2] p. 206, Turner[2] p. 109, and Brenk p. 45ff.). In the soldier's case, it is a self-imposed exclusion caused by his moral scruples, lacks in consequence the usual threat of violence to the door (cf. *Old*

own emotions; or (3) it marks the remnants of a suggestion by Getas that Krateia has attracted the attention of someone else (Katsouris[2] p. 209). But if this is so, how are we to interpret the reaction that follows, if the attribution to Thrasonides is correct? One possible solution lies perhaps in reinterpretation of the Greek as a reference to the soldier: '*Getas:* What, a magnetic personality like you?' In this way the slave might attempt to dismiss his master's view of Krateia's behaviour and to continue his reassessment in the lines that follow.

A50ff. I wait.... Do wait a bit': Despite their ostensible clarity, interpretation of the lines is fraught with difficulty. Is Thrasonides referring to an actual occurrence or merely romancing? Is his description, with its use of the present tense ostensibly for vividness, relevant to that very night (note the similarity of weather conditions), a mark of his attempt to break through Krateia's reserve after his recent return, or does it point to an altogether longer timescale and a repeated ploy (contrast Brown p. 5, and Katsouris[2] p. 210f.)?

A95. Damn you!: Exasperation that for all Thrasonides' anxiety and frustration Getas can apparently offer little beyond damning his master with seemingly ironic faint praise.

Fragments cited by ancient authors which have some bearing on the play's exposition and are perhaps relevant to Acts I or II:

1. Choricius xlii, *Decl.* 12: (see above A43 n.)
2. Arrian *Diss. Epicteti* IV, 1, 19: 'See what Thrasonides says and does.... First he comes out of doors at night when Getas doesn't dare come.... Then he says 'A paltry little wench has enslaved me, something no enemy has ever done'.... Then he asks for a sword and gets angry when the other character, motivated by goodwill, refuses to give him one, and he sends gifts to the girl who hates him and he begs and weeps. Then, once he has had some slight success, he becomes excited.'
3. Scholion on *Odyssey* XVII 422: 'He did very well out of Cyprus, since he was in the service of one of the kings there.'
4. Pollux X 145: 'The swords have disappeared.'

In addition to these there exists a further scrap of papyrus which may belong to Act I, though its precise location within the action remains a source of contention. In it, after references to a female's absence and the name Getas, a character says: 'Apollo! How very soldierly!... Now, as you see, I'm going indoors...muggers by walking about and escaping them in a relaxed manner...'. One suggested context is as variant to the standard introduction of the chorus at the end of Act I. Others prefer a location after 56; others still, with perhaps more justice, would set it at the end of the opening scene and follow it with the necessary divine prologue, but certainty is impossible.

Act III

After the extreme fragmentation of Act II, the third Act opens with further problems as to who is speaking and the topic of their conversation. From the evidence of 132, 'are you going to fight with me?', the characters involved would seem to be at odds with one another, and since their dialogue ostensibly centres on the rift between Thrasonides, now 'living a terribly miserable life', and Krateia, the subject perhaps of 'She knows her own business best', they may well be servants attached to each of the principal characters. One of them, certainly, is female, since the Greek word translated 'Oh dear' in 132 is only used by women. An alternative interpretation favoured by some editors, however, would make the exchange after 'Saying what?' direct quotation of offstage dialogue. How, though, are we to interpret 'Off with you' in 141 (the Greek does not make clear how many people are involved) and 'Let's go' at 155, where the text again becomes too fragmentary to make much sense? Does the first mark the departure of one of the speakers, leaving the other to soliloquise or address a mute attendant, or is it followed by a fresh entry and dialogue before the exit at 155, part of the rapid turnover of stage personnel which seems to characterise Act III? And what are we to make of the letters 'RY' in the margin at 155? They clearly mark the remains of a speaker's name, but is there much point in hypothesising a Chrysis, Phrygia or Tryphe?

160. A man sang: No completely satisfactory explanation has yet been offered which allows us to identify the man referred to here, establish the event's location, or even glimpse the dramatic significance of the speech. In terms of identity, both Demeas and Kleinias would seem to be ruled out, the former since Getas shows no sign of recognising the man he accosts at 216ff., unless his remark at 218 ('this is the chap I've been looking for') points to the passage here, a continuation of the suspicion the singer evidently aroused in the slave. Was it in fact the man – Demeas – who was trying 'to watch the woman from outside', part of an attempt to discover if she was his daughter? Kleinias, in turn, seems ruled out, in that he arrives to organise his own party at 270ff. Furthermore, since the man in question was not alone, who is 'the other' referred to at 164? All that we can perhaps say, is that the fat-faced man seems to be acquainted with Thrasonides – hence the question at 171f. – and the whole incident may represent the soldier's attempt to deflect his misery with high living (cf. Charisios in *The Arbitration*). There are, however, so many imponderables in Getas' speech that any attempt to integrate it into the plot seems doomed to founder in a sea of conjecture.

176. such a peculiar visitor: Demeas, who seems to be the subject of similar references elsewhere (31, not given in the translation, 273, 286, 325). His interest in the soldier's swords, stored for the moment in Kleinias' house (see above fr. 2), now comes to the fore and is explained by 'I recognise this sword as my own' in 193.

188. Knock at the door: Why does Demeas ask the old woman to knock at Thrasonides' door for him rather than do it himself? Does he have qualms about approaching the soldier in person, as the translation's restoration 'It's awkward' suggests, or is it a device to heighten tension in readiness for events to come? And why, when he does eventually knock, does he then move away from the door when there is an immediate response? Sandbach[1] advances the technical necessity of avoiding a crowded doorway scene, as first Krateia and her nurse appear, followed at 216 by Getas. Others point to the close connection between the knocking and the door opening, suggesting that the old man realises this new figure appears for reasons of her own, not in response to his summons. Such a scenario is not, however, without its own illogicality, as Krateia emerges unaware that there has been any knocking at all. Is this, in fact, an instance of Menander's readiness to overstep the bounds of logic in order to attain the effects he wants: (1) an unexpected confrontation, such as playwrights had often striven to produce (cf. Orestes and Clytemnestra in Aeschylus' *Libation Bearers* 668); or (2) the creation of further tension through momentary delay before the emotion of the recognition scene?

208f. I couldn't have...a moment longer!...: Various explanations have been offered to account for Krateia's words here, usually based on her supposed desire either to escape the soldier or to meet her father. The latter is itself founded on the supposition that the nurse had been on stage earlier in the Act, was identical in fact with one of the female figures already seen, and had recognised Demeas (cf. Sandbach[1] p. 450). Needless to say there is nothing in the extant text to provide any justification for such ideas.

210. The thought never entered my head...: lit. 'What *unexpected* sight do I see?' It is difficult to reconcile Demeas' astonishment here at being suddenly confronted by his daughter, with the view that the tattered remains in Act II provide him with evidence of Krateia's presence in Thrasonides' house.

211. What do you mean, Nurse?: By skilful use of a mute to play the nurse, Menander is able to overcome the limitations imposed on him by the conventional restriction of speaking parts to three: Krateia, Demeas and Getas. To do this, he first represents the two women as if in mid-conversation when they enter and with the nurse's revelation covered by Demeas' exclamation in 210. He then puts words into her mouth when Krateia proceeds to repeat the substance of her statement. From this, in turn, the recognition itself flows with natural ease. Why, though, do we find no enquiry from either side as to how the other came to be there? Is it simply to avoid a slackening in the pace of the action, or are the fleeting references to letters in the highly fragmentary remains between A100 and Act III relevant here?

216. what's this?: Getas' reaction to the sight of father and daughter together allows Menander to inject an element of mild humour, which serves to separate the elation of discovery from the depths of despair that are to come.

218. this is the chap I've been looking for: What is the significance of the words? Do they refer to something in the slave's speech at 160ff., or are they confirmation of Getas' belief in a rival lover as the cause of Krateia's coldness towards Thrasonides (cf. A43 n., Katsouris[2] p. 223)?

230. I wish I had: i.e., Demeas no longer has a home in Cyprus to come from. This does not mean, however, that Demeas is a native of Cyprus. Since the aim of the play is doubtless a marriage for his daughter, he is probably an Athenian who, for one reason or another, has chosen to live on the island.

246ff. If he's no longer alive: It is one of the great misfortunes for our understanding of the play that a scene which might have explained so much about previous developments has survived in only fragmentary form, and in two separate versions which pose more questions than they provide answers. As given in the translation, it is Demeas who seemingly reveals the awful truth concerning the death of someone we may presume is Krateia's brother (though this fact is never stated as such in the text). The scenario suggested by the alternative source and favoured by a number of editors would produce in contrast: '*Krateia*: …Father dear. *Demeas*: Is he dead? *Krateia*: At the hands of… *Demeas*: Do you know who it was? *Krateia*: I do. I was…'. Add to this the possibility of textual corruption or alternative punctuation and the range of possibility expands still further (cf. Sandbach[1] p. 452f., and Katsouris[2] p. 224 n.1), though clearly a system which allows both father and daughter to contribute information equally and reveals that Krateia's earlier coldness towards the soldier was not caused simply by his boasting has definite attractions. All that we can say for certain, however, is that the conclusion reached here must ultimately prove false, since the play could no more contain a death so close to the heart of the action and remain a comedy than could *The Shield*. As the Act nears its close the playwright foreshadows the clash of wills reported in Act IV by the juxtaposition of intention on the part of father and daughter here, and expectations of trouble from Thrasonides at 259ff. Such premonitions of disaster from the soldier also allow insertion of dramatic irony on a number of levels for an audience which knows how justified they are, but realises that ultimately all will be well.

270ff. Kleinias: On a technical level, the introduction of this brief scene provides in the person of Kleinias that bridge between Acts already seen at work in other plays of Menander. Thematically, on the other hand, it seems to refer to some strand in the action of which we know nothing else. Similarly, the passing mention of the cook may have been introduced as preparation for the inevitable celebrations at the end of the play (cf. 450 n.) or simply to remind the audience of the humour normally associated with such a figure, and thus to round off the Act on a less than gloomy note (cf. Turner[1] p. 13ff.). Of the other characters referred to the visitor must be Demeas, but who is the woman? Speculation that she may be Krateia, who Kleinias believes intends to leave the soldier and hopes will take refuge with him, remains just that, speculation (for the edifices of restoration built on the lines see Katsouris[2] p. 224 n.2).

Act IV

Despite the relative brevity of the text in Act IV, restricted as it is to virtually a single scene, the plot clearly proceeds to its crisis point, and then, on the analogy of other Menandrean plays, to its resolution. Yet if we are correct in assuming that the death Demeas and Krateia believe has occurred involves the girl's brother, how exactly is the resolution effected? The plot of *The Shield* offers an immediate and ostensibly compelling answer, but if that is the case, from where does the brother emerge and how? Some have suggested that he may turn out to be Kleinias, but this immediately raises a number of further difficulties:

1) Since Demeas is apparently Kleinias' guest, why have the two not recognised one another already, especially when 231ff. implies that the old man's family has only recently been scattered by war? Does the answer lie in the opening speech of the Act, the fact that Kleinias seemingly knows nothing of the swords deposited in his house, which suggests he may have been away for some considerable time and not yet met his guest? How though could Kleinias ever become host to someone without prior acquaintance?

2) Is the loss of the brother altogether unconnected with the recent

war, the result instead of kidnapping in youth, or is he merely a half-brother of Krateia, the product of some irregular union, with whom Demeas left the sword as a token of identity (see further Sandbach[1] p. 440f.)?

3) Does the sword that Demeas has recognised (178ff., 276) really belong to Thrasonides, or is it one of Kleinias' which has become mixed up with those of the soldier? Certainly the text at 276, lit. 'lying in our house' not 'left...' as the translation suggests, may carry such an implication, especially in view of the reference to '*the* sword' not '*a* sword', which we might have expected from 178. It should be abundantly clear, however, that we are now in the realm not of fact but of hypothesis. To go further, to delve into alternative scenarios for which there is even less evidence in the Greek, would merely add further floors to an already precarious house of cards.

280. woman: lit. 'old woman', i.e., the one who appeared at 176.

284ff. Getas: The slave's entry brings with it the results of Krateia's earlier determination to formulate a plan of action against Thrasonides. But whereas the events described are essentially serious, Menander balances this with the visual comedy of Getas ignoring both Kleinias' enquiries and his presence as he follows the slave round the stage, something Bain[1] p. 141f. regards as worthy of Plautine farce and a parody of standard comic convention. In some ways, indeed, the scene has affinities with *The Shield* 399ff., though there Daos' failure to see Smikrines was deliberate. The injection of Kleinias' asides and comments also provides a further instance of Menander's tendency to break up lengthy narrative into manageable sections: first Thrasonides' pleas, then the interaction of father and soldier with their contrasting requests – that from Demeas marked by its emphatic brusqueness ('The only answer...') – and finally Thrasonides' appeals to Krateia, surrounded as they are by actions from her deliberately calculated to snub him ('*She* looked away again...She didn't even answer him').

303. wild boar on the mountain: The precise significance is unknown, but in the context of Demeas' refusal to consider Thrasonides' proposal, and his insistence upon purchasing the freedom of his daughter, it probably corresponds to 'pig-headed'.

307. I had the name of being your first lover: Is the wording here significant? By stressing the implication that Thrasonides was a lover in name only, some have suggested that Krateia remains a virgin in readiness for her eventual marriage. Support for such an idea may come from the presumption that the soldier has only recently gained possession of her. On the other hand, the claim at A40 ('thought of her as my wife') and the description at A50ff., like the situation upon which *The Rape of the Locks* is based, might well be used to reach a totally different conclusion.

315. *I* wouldn't have ransomed her: Getas' reaction suggests Thrasonides has acceded to Demeas' request and handed Krateia over to him, but without any reciprocal agreement on the question of marriage. From this, the slave launches into what seems to be an imaginary dialogue, based ostensibly on how he would have behaved had he been in his master's shoes. The passage, however, is beset by problems of interpretation, not least the number of speakers involved. So for instance, while 'And when you two...to you either' is unquestionably plural and should presumably refer to Demeas and Krateia, we cannot be sure who is addressed by the singular 'You have none?' or even if this is the correct interpretation of the Greek. Is Getas now restricting his imaginary dialogue to Demeas alone, has he changed addressee altogether, or is he merely quoting the words of someone else? And what is the relationship between this and what follows, 'He'll rant...'? Commentators have been tempted to take refuge in the belief that by varying tone and gesture an actor could make everything clear in performance, and as a result have proposed schemes of considerable complexity (cf. Blundell p. 76ff.). That the premise is without foundation, however, needs little demonstration.

320f. he'll plan to kill himself: This is presumably a reference to Thrasonides, who in fr. 2 (see above) had asked for a sword, apparently with this in mind (cf. 309f.).

324f. My visitor...to you: As with 286f., the banality of Kleinias' remark contrasts strongly with the tone of Getas' outpourings.

388. Are you acting as her advocate?: Like the admission of love in 360, these scraps of Thrasonides' soliloquy bear all the hallmarks of an inward struggle to reconcile his attachment to Krateia with her rejection of him, and to keep his predicament secret while finding a way out of it. In the fragments of Greek text that follow 390 we find further references to giving up life, ill-treatment by Krateia despite kindnesses, an examination perhaps of Thrasonides' way of life and the unlikelihood of Krateia's hatred being softened.

Act V

As Miller notes, the remains of Act V, which consist of half-lines at best, allow restoration of the obligatory happy ending but little else.

431. They are giving you your wife...: Demeas must be one of those mentioned here since in law he was the only person capable of betrothing his daughter. The other is presumably the lost brother.

434. You're not playing tricks?...: cf. *The Arbitration* 954 n., *The Rape of the Locks* 990.

439. Yes, Daddy...: The direct quotation of Krateia's words is important, signifying her personal acceptance of a husband rather than simple compliance with her father's wishes and thus the restoration of the love motif (cf. *The Rape of the Locks* 1006ff.).

446. a handsome dowry: lit. two talents (12,000 drachmas) as in *The Shield* 135, but how had Demeas' fortune survived a war that had scattered his household? Was it in fact the brother who provided the dowry?

450. ...dinner for all...: The celebration that marks the end of the play doubtless made good use of the cook introduced as a passing reference by Kleinias at 270.

459ff.: On the closing formula compare *Old Cantankerous*, *The Girl from Samos* and *The Sikyonian*. As always, the appeal 'Ladies and Gentlemen' is directed in the Greek to the male members of the audience only (cf. *Old Cantankerous* 194 n.).

Unassigned fragments:

5. [Justin] *De Monarchia* 5: 'If I were to see this, I would even get my spirits back. As it is – but where can one find the gods so just, Getas?'
6. Scholion on Aristophanes' *Thesmophoriazusae* 423: 'I think I'll have to carry round a Spartan key.' (This locked the door from the outside, cf. Plautus' *The Ghost* 403f.)

The Double Deceiver

Act II

The importance of *The Double Deceiver* lies not so much in its intrinsic merits, interesting as the fragments of the play are, but in the light these shed on the adaptation produced by the Roman playwright Plautus in the composition of his own work, *The Two Bacchises*. Before discovery of the fragments the greatest overlap between a Greek original and its Roman counterpart had consisted of three passages, a total of just over 31 lines, from Menander's *Plokion* (*The Little Necklace*, see translation p. 240ff.) later used by Caecilius Statius, who was active in the period between Plautus and Terence (i.e., c.184-166 BC) but of whose work not so much as a scene survives. As Miller's Introduction points out, comparison of the relevant passages from *The Double Deceiver* and *The Two Bacchises* now allows us to gauge the extent to which Plautus altered his Greek model in terms of title, character names, metre, structure and comic tone to suit both his audience and the conventions of the Roman stage (see further Handley[2], Sandbach[1] p. 118ff., Arnott[4] p. 140ff., Bain[2]). In addition to direct comparison of the two plays in dramatic terms, however, our ability to set them side by side also provides a control mechanism for questions of textual restoration and emendation which is not without its own significance for Plautine scholarship as a whole.

11. Get him out: Moschos' father instructs Sostratos to rescue his son from the clutches of the young man's present girlfriend, someone Sostratos believes to be the girl he himself fell for in Ephesus, but who is, in fact, her twin sister. Though the Greek text is defective in this and the next line, Menander has apparently aimed for particular stylistic effect through the introduction of *tricolon*, in this case three commands set one after another. This the Plautine version replaces (in the Latin) with the sonorous effect of assonance, alliteration and repeated word order. In 16 ('Go for him...him') the reverse occurs, with Plautus replacing Menander's two

135

verbs with three (497 'take over, go and dress him down properly'). It is also in 16 that we see the first instance of one version correcting another. The traditional Latin text of 497ff. ('Mnesilochus...dissolute behaviour') assigned the lines to Philoxenus. Menander on the other hand gives them to Lydos, vindicating the assignment suggested by Hermann in 1845. Similarly, it has been usual for editors of Plautus to place 496 of *The Two Bacchises* ('Then I'm leaving...I'm coming') at the very end of the scene on the evidence of the oldest manuscript, the Ambrosian palimpsest written in the third or fourth century AD. Discovery of the Menandrean scenes now shows clearly where the line correctly belongs, justifying an alternative strand of the manuscript tradition. One further instance of textual correction in these lines, worth mentioning, again demonstrates that a manuscript's priority in terms of age does not necessarily guarantee a superior version in all cases. By reference to Menander, it is now clear that the text of 498 proposed by some editors of Plautus on the basis of the Ambrosian palimpsest ('a perfect disgrace to you, me, his friend, and others') can no longer be defended against the alternative given in the translation (see further Handley[2] p. 10).

18ff. Well, that does for Moschos: Sostratos' agitation is well indicated by the disjointed statements he makes, as he piles one thought on top of another without much concern for coherence, and alternates references to the girl by means of both 'she' and 'you'. The text in the monologue is, in fact, more fragmentary than the translation suggests, with notable omissions in 25, lit. 'let her try her wiles on [a man with empty pockets] who has nothing', and 29 'conversing...[with a corpse]'. Supplementation in the case of the first is helped both by repetition of the phrasing at 92 ('my pockets are empty') and by the evidence of Plautus at 517 ('when my pockets are empty'). In the case of the second instance restoration takes its cue from Plautus' use of the motif at 518 ('prattling away at a dead man's grave'). In other respects, however, comparison of the Menandrean and Plautine versions reveals a considerable shift in emphasis, with the latter undergoing considerable expansion by the insertion of comic banter which in itself serves to indicate the different priorities of the two playwrights. While Menander, for instance, strives to maintain the logicality of his characters and the situation in which they find themselves, Plautus is fully prepared to interrupt the flow of the play with comic material that both delays, and in some respects, contradicts, the rationale of events (505-10). On the other hand, the quips that he injects employ the same technique we saw earlier in Menander at *Old Cantankerous* 661, 669: altering the expected sense of a statement by use of some significant word or phrase at its very end; so for instance, 'love her' (505), 'rob my father' (507), 'for my father' (508). That Mnesilochus' musings here are indeed irrelevant is shown by the way he brings them to an end: 'But I must be clean out of my mind, maundering on here like this...'.

26f. I'll give the money to my father: Sostratos' motive in taking this course of action seems to be a mixture of wanting to avenge himself on the girl and a genuine desire to keep the money safe, since he realises that he is like putty in her hands (hence the bluster in 91ff., followed by the clue to his true feelings from Moschos at 105 'There are even tears in your eyes'). Plautus, in contrast, gives greater prominence to the theme of revenge, as Bacchis dominates virtually the whole speech.

50. your good friend: The man in Ephesus with whom the money was originally deposited and from whom it was now being fetched. According to the story outlined in Plautus, he had denied ever receiving the money, had given it up only after a court case, and had then conspired with pirates to seize it back. It was this plot that had supposedly necessitated its deposit with the fictitious Theotimos. As Miller observes, this dialogue, like that which opens Act III, is entirely omitted by Plautus. Instead, lacking as he did the convention of the choral interlude, the playwright was forced to use other means to cover the return of the money (cf. 91ff. n.).

53. You'll get it: Sostratos is unable to hand the money over immediately since it had been hidden on his arrival, part of the plot devised by Syros to finance the young man's love affair.

58. Syros: In changing the slave's name to Chrysalus (Goldie) Plautus injects an additional element of appropriateness for a character whose function is the diversion of funds. Later, at 649f., the playwright develops this further with an observation that has all the semblance of a private joke placed into the mouth of the slave: 'I don't care for your Parmenos and *Syruses* who twist two or three minae (200-300 drachmas) from their masters'.

63. *That* matters to me more than anything: The anxiety of Sostratos' father to get his money, already signalled in 52 and 61, may foreshadow an overall unsympathetic portrayal of him in readiness for later deception. Opposite the line, in the margin of the papyrus, occurs the Greek numeral 364, which has been interpreted as marking either the total number of lines copied in the play up to that point, or merely the total number in the Act. The latter view is favoured by Turner[1] p. 223ff. (cf. Arnott[4] p. 142, and Sandbach[1]) who argues (1) that the alternative, based on the total in Acts I and II, would produce a wide discrepancy between Menander with 364 lines and Plautus with 525; and (2) that line 108 of the Roman play ('Follow me indoors and lie down so you can get rid of your weariness') seems to denote what in the Greek original would have been the end of Act I. The result for Plautus' version is a second 'Act' 417 lines long, which provides a far greater degree of parity with the Greek figure. At the same time, however, we need to recognise that Turner's explanation results in an Act longer than any other in Menander's surviving works, and that the calculation is based on an interpretation of the manuscript figure's significance which remains contentious. Still further complication arises from the recent suggestion that the Acts involved are in fact III and IV.

Act III

91ff. And now that my pockets are empty: Once again Menander bridges the gap between Acts by reintroducing stage personnel and themes already developed, as Sostratos echoes much of the monologue he delivered at 19ff. To this he then adds the theme of betrayal by Moschos, natural under the circumstances, but immediately given an ironic twist as Sostratos chooses to view his friend not as the initiating agent in the deception but as the victim of his girlfriend's wiles (cf. Demeas' interpretation of Chrysis' role in *The Girl from Samos*). This aspect of the speech is altogether absent from the Plautine version, and for obvious reasons. Not only has the abandonment of choral interludes necessitated a reversed order of entrance, with Pistoclerus appearing first in order to allow time for the money to be handed over, but the young man's presence already on stage makes any reference to betrayal by him in Mnesilochus' monologue at 530ff. impossible.

102f. Then if he knows...: Moschos' opening words provide the briefest of reasons for his arrival on stage. This is in stark contrast to Pistoclerus' entrance monologue at 526ff., which was clearly designed not only to cover Mnesilochus' absence but also to provide the audience with a clear reminder of Pistoclerus' identity and the circumstances surrounding his reappearance. Further expansion of the Menandrean model occurs in the preliminaries to the actual charge of betrayal, as both young men engage in protracted verbal shadow-boxing (cf. Bain[1] p. 142ff.,[2] p. 24ff.). Part of this involves Mnesilochus' use of a hypothetical third party in place of any direct reference to Pistoclerus, a feature some commentators have regarded as superior to Menander's technique in that it allows a greater build-up of tension, especially when Pistoclerus is shown to agree with his friend at 540ff. How valid such a judgement is, however, in the context of the scene as a whole remains a matter of debate (see further Bain[2] p. 29ff.).

Unassigned fragments:

1. Papyrus IFAO 337: 'In God's name, young man' (the words are attributed by restoration to the play's beginning, suggesting a dialogue – see further Arnott[4] p. 151ff.).
2. Fulgentius *Mythologiae* III, i: 'Like a counsellor you anticipated our own impression, Demeas.'
3. Bekker *Anecdota* I, 436, 17: 'Stand beside me. I'll knock at the door and summon one of them' (cf. *The Two Bacchises* 810, 1117).
4. Stobaeus *Eclogae* IV, 52, 27: 'He whom the gods love, dies young' (cf. *The Two Bacchises* 816f.).
5. Photius, Suda, Etymologicum Genuinum: 'It was not Megabyzos who became temple warden'. (Megabyzos was the family name of the temple warden in Ephesus. Though no exact parallel exists in *The Two Bacchises*, Arnott[4] p. 171 points to 306-13 as a possible context.)

Bibliography

Anderson, M., 'Knemon's Hamartia', *Greece & Rome* 17 (1970) pp. 199-217.

Anderson, W.S., (1) 'A New Menandrian Prototype for the *Servus Currens* of Roman Comedy', *Phoenix* 24 (1970) pp. 229-36.

———— (2) 'The Ending of the *Samia* and Other Menandrian Comedies', in *Studi classici in onore di Quinto Cataudella II* (Catania, 1972) pp. 155-79.

Arnott, W.G., (1) 'The Confrontation of Sostratos and Gorgias', *Phoenix* 18 (1964) pp. 110-23.

———— (2) 'Menander, Qui Vitae Ostendit Vitam', *Greece & Rome* 15 (1968) pp. 1-17.

———— (3) 'The Modernity of Menander', *Greece & Rome* 22 (1975) pp. 140-55.

———— (4) *Menander* I (London, 1979).

———— (5) 'Time, Plot and Character in Menander', *Papers of the Liverpool Latin Seminar II* Cairns, F. (ed.), (Liverpool, 1979) pp. 343-60.

———— (6) 'Moral Values in Menander', *Philologus* 125 (1981) pp. 215-27.

———— (7) 'Menander and Earlier Drama', in *Studies in Honour of T.B.L.Webster I*, Betts, J.H., *et al.* (eds), (Bristol, 1986) pp. 1-9.

———— (8) 'The Time-Scale of Menander's *Epitrepontes, Zeitschrift für Papyrologie und Epigraphik*' 70 (1987) pp. 19-31.

———— (9) 'New Evidence for the Opening of Menander's *Perikeiromene*?', *Zeitschrift für Papyrologie und Epigraphik* 71 (1988) pp. 11-15.

———— (10) 'Gorgias' Exit at Menander, *Dyskolos* 381-92', *Zeitschrift für Papyrologie und Epigraphik* 76 (1989) pp. 3-5.

———— (11) 'A Study in Relationships, Alexis' *Lebes*, Menander's *Dyskolos*, Plautus' *Aulularia*', *Quaderni Urbinati di Cultura Classica* 33.3 (1989) pp. 27-38.

Bader, E., 'The ψόφος of the House Door in Greek New Comedy', *Antichthon* 5 (1971) pp. 35-48.

Bain D., (1) *Actors and Audience: A Study of Asides and Related Conventions in Greek Drama* (Oxford, 1977).

———— (2) 'Plautus Vortit Barbare', in *Creative Imitation and Latin Literature*, West, D., and Woodman, T. (eds) (Cambridge, 1979) pp. 17-34.

———— (3) *Menander Samia* (Warminster, 1983).

Blundell, J., *Menander and the Monologue*, Hypomnemata 59 (Göttingen, 1980).

Brenk, F.E., '*Heteros tis eimi*: On the Language of Menander's Young Lovers, *Illinois Classical Studies* 12 (1987) pp. 33-66.

Brown, P.G. McC., 'The Beginning of the *Misoumenos*', (review of E.G. Turner, *The Lost Beginning of Menander* Misoumenos, London, 1977) *Classical Review* 30 (1980) pp. 3-6.

Dedoussi, C., 'The Future of Plangon's Child in Menander's *Samia*', *Liverpool Classical Monthly* 13 (1988) pp. 39-42.

Dover, K.J., *Greek Popular Morality in the Time of Plato and Aristotle* (Oxford, 1974).

Dworaki, S., 'The Prologues in the Comedies of Menander', *Eos* 61 (1973) pp. 33-47.

Fantham, E., 'Sex, Status, and Survival in Hellenistic Athens: A Study of Women in New Comedy', *Phoenix* 29 (1975) pp. 44-74.

Fisher, N.R.E., *Social Values in Classical Athens* (London, 1976).

Fortenbaugh, W.W., 'Menander's *Perikeiromene*: Misfortune, Vehemence and Polemon', *Phoenix* 28 (1974) pp. 430-43.

Frost, K.B., *Exits and Entrances in Menander* (Oxford, 1988).

Goldberg, S.M., (1) 'The Style and Function of Menander's *Dyskolos* Prologue', *Symbolae Osloenses* 53 (1978) pp. 57-68.

———— (2) *The Making of Menander's Comedy* (London, 1980).

Grant, J.N., The Father-Son Relationship and the Ending of Menander's *Samia, Phoenix* 40 (1986) pp. 172-84.

Groton, A.H., 'Anger in Menander's *Samia*', *American Journal of Philology* 108 (1987) pp. 437-43.

Handley E.W., (1) *The* Dyskolos *of Menander* (London, 1965).

———— (2) *Menander and Plautus: A Study in Comparison* (London, 1968).

Harrison, A.R.W., *The Law of Athens: The Family and Property* (Oxford, 1968).

Henry, M.H., *Menander's Courtesans and the Greek Comic Tradition* (Frankfurt, 1985).

Ireland, S. (1) 'Menander and the Comedy of Disappointment', *Liverpool Classical Monthly* 8 (1983) pp. 45-7.

———— (2) *Terence, The Mother-in-Law* (Warminster, 1990).

Jacques, J-M., *Ménandre, La Samienne* (Paris, 1971).

Katsouris, A.G., (1) *Tragic Patterns in Menander* (Athens, 1975).

———— (2) 'Menander's *Misoumenos*: Problems of Interpretation', *Dodone* 14 (1985) pp. 205-29.

Keuls, E., (1) 'Mystery Elements in Menander's *Dyskolos*', *Transactions of the American Philological Association* 100 (1969) pp. 209-20.

———— (2) 'The *Samia* of Menander, an Interpretation of its Plot and Theme', *Zeitschrift für Papyrologie und Epigraphik* 10 (1973) pp. 1-20.

Lloyd-Jones, H., (1) 'Menander's *Sikyonios*', *Greek, Roman and Byzantine Studies* 7 (1966) pp. 131-57.

———— (2) 'Menander's *Aspis*', *Greek, Roman and Byzantine Studies* 12 (1971) pp. 175-95.

Lombard, D.B., 'New Values in Traditional Forms. A Study in Menander's *Aspis*', *Acta Classica* 14 (1971) pp. 123-45.

MacCary, W.T., (1) 'Menander's Slaves: Their Names, Roles and Masks', *Transactions of the American Philological Association* 100 (1969) pp. 277-94.

———— (2) 'Menander's Old Men', *Transactions of the American Philological Association* 102 (1971) pp. 303-25.

———— (3) 'Menander's Soldiers: Their Names, Roles, and Masks', *American Journal of Philology* 93 (1972) pp. 279-98.

MacDowell, D.M., (1) 'Hybris in Athens', *Greece & Rome* 23 (1976) pp. 14-31.

———— (2) 'Love Versus the Law. An Essay on Menander's *Aspis*', *Greece & Rome* 29 (1982) pp. 42-52.

Ramage, E.S., 'City and Country in Menander's *Dyskolos*', *Philologus* 110 (1966) pp. 194-211.

Sandbach, F.H., (1) *Menander, a Commentary*, Gomme, A.W., and Sandbach, F.H. (Oxford, 1973).

———— (2) 'Two Notes on Menander (*Epitrepontes* and *Samia*)', *Liverpool Classical Monthly* 11 (1986) pp. 156-60.

Turner, E.G., (1) *Ménandre*, Entretiens sur l'Antiquité Classique 16, Fondation Hardt (Geneva, 1970).

———— (2) 'Menander and the New Society of His Time', *Chronique d'Egypte* 54 (1979) pp. 106-26.

Webster, T.B.L., (1) *Studies in Menander*, 2nd edn (Manchester, 1960).

———— (2) *An Introduction to Menander* (Manchester, 1974).

West, S., 'Notes on the Samia', *Zeitschrift für Papyrologie und Epigraphik* 88 (1991) pp. 11-23.

Zagagi, N., (1) *Tradition and Originality in Plautus*, Hypomnemata 62 (Gottingen, 1980).

———— (2) 'Divine Interventions and Human Agents in Menander', in *Relire Ménandre*, Handley, E. and Hurst, A., (eds) (Geneva, 1990) pp. 63-91.

Supplementary List of Items not included in the Commentary

Arnott, W.G., *Menander, Plautus, Terence*, Greece & Rome New Surveys in the Classics 9 (Oxford, 1975).

Hunter, R.L., *The New Comedy of Greece and Rome* (Cambridge, 1985).

Katsouris, A.G., 'Menander's Techniques for Lowering Tension', *Liverpool Classical Monthly* 8 (1983) pp. 30-1.

MacCary, W.T., 'Menander's Characters, Their Names, Roles and Masks', *Transactions of the American Philological Association* 101 (1970) pp. 277-90.

Sandbach, F.H., *The Comic Theatre of Greece and Rome* (London, 1977).

Index

OC: Old Cantankerous
GGS: The Girl From Samos
A: The Arbitration
RL: The Rape of the Locks
Sh: The Shield
Sik: The Sikyonian
MH: The Man She Hated
DD: The Double Deceiver

[References to Acts refer to the general observations that precede individual notes]